# Javanese Justice and the Soul of Indonesia

A Lawyer's Guide to Culture, Law, and the Hopes of His Nation

JAVANESE JUSTICE AND THE SOUL OF INDONESIA A LAWYER'S GUIDE TO CULTURE, LAW, AND THE HOPES OF HIS NATION

**First edition. August 1, 2025.**



ISBN: 979-8231614561

Written by Muhammad Ari Pratomo.

To those who still believe in justice with a soul.

To the Javanese culture that raised me,the law that shaped me,and the people who never stopped hoping.

For my child—whose name I whisper in every prayer,and whose future I want to help protect through every word I write.

And to the silent ones,whose voices were unheard,whose stories were ignored—may this book be part of your echo.

*"When tradition whispers and justice listens, a lawyer finds his truest voice."*— Muhammad Ari Pratomo

# Muhammad Ari Pratomo

Published By :
PT MuhammadAriLaw Pustaka Nada
Citra Indah City Housing Complex, Bukit Azalea AF 7 No. 3
Jonggol, Bogor Regency
Website: www.mpnpublishing.com
E-mail:admin@mpnpublishing.com
Tel.: +628115222152

Book title

# Javanese Justice and the Soul of Indonesia

A Lawyer's Guide to Culture, Law, and the Hopes of His Nation

**Writer**

Muhammad Ari Pratomo

**Editor**

Muhammad Ari Pratomo

**Layout Designer, Front and Back Cover**

Muhammad Ari Pratomo

Pages: iv + 117 ; 14.8 cm x 21 cm

ISBN :

QRCBN :

Edition: August 1, 2, 2025

**Publisher:**

PT MuhammadAriLaw Pustaka Nada

Citra Indah City Housing Complex, Bukit Azalea AF 7 No. 3 Jonggol, Bogor Regency

Website: www.mpnpublishing.com

E-mail:admin@mpnpublishing.com

Tel.:

+628115222152

# FOREWORD

This book was born from my long journey as a lawyer, writer, and citizen who constantly questions: can the law truly side with the people if it is cut off from its own cultural roots?

As a Javanese child raised in oral traditions, local wisdom, and wayang stories, I believe that justice exists not only in the courtroom. It lives in songs, in social practices, and in philosophies passed down from generation to generation. However, in the midst of rapid modernity, many of these meanings have been eroded, even forgotten.

Through this book, I try to re-assemble the relationship between culture and law, between the traditional narratives that shape the soul of the nation, and the legal system that regulates our lives today.

I invite readers from various backgrounds, including those in the legal world, academics, cultural practitioners, and the younger generation, to re-explore the soul of Indonesia through a rarely touched-upon perspective: the intersection of justice, identity, and culture.

Hopefully this book will be a small way to bring the law closer to humanity, and humanity to more meaningful justice.

**Muhammad Ari Pratomo**

**List of contents**

# CHAPTER 1

## Tracing the Traces of Law in Ancestral Land

No law is born in a vacuum. Law, like culture, is a reflection of a nation's collective soul. In Java, where I was born and raised, law is more than just a set of rigid rules. It lives in behavior, speech, and everyday symbols that we often don't even recognize as law.

Since childhood, I've seen how the elders in the village resolve problems without going to the police station. Some were resolved through mediation at the hamlet head's house, while others simply sat together in the pavilion over tea. Everything was done politely, respectfully, and sometimes interspersed with a few comforting jokes.

This is where I first learned that justice doesn't always come in the form of a black and white verdict. Sometimes it comes in silence, sometimes in a sincere smile. Javanese law is unhurried. It considers feelings, not just the article. It maintains harmony, not just imposes sanctions.

However, over time, I also saw a growing clash between state law and local wisdom. When the law dictates one thing, but custom dictates another. When authorities demand obedience, but citizens demand more humane justice. Amidst all of this, I grew up as a restless young man. Wanting to be part of the system, but also wanting to stay rooted.

Becoming a lawyer was a conscious choice. But being a lawyer who upholds cultural values is an ongoing struggle.

I learned that local wisdom is not a barrier to progress. It is the inner foundation that keeps the law from losing its way. Without it, the law can be cold and sharp, but soulless.

In the following chapters, I will share stories, reflections, and contemplations about how Javanese culture shapes our perspectives on law, justice, and hope. This is not a theoretical book. It is the record of a child of the nation who believes that law can be a path home to our own souls.

I still remember an incident when a village elder was visited by two families disputing over a land boundary. There was no lawyer, no judge. Just an old map, two cups of tea, and the elder's low, authoritative voice: "Don't chase victory if it means sacrificing peace."

Those words echoed in my mind, even as I sat in the courtroom, surrounded by files, articles, and conflicts that had lost their warmth. I often asked myself: "Do we still have room to resolve problems with emotion, not just logic?"

My journey as an advocate has brought me into contact with a wide variety of clients, from ordinary citizens to public figures. Interestingly, almost all of them came with the same pain: the feeling that the law was too distant, too cold, too complicated. This is where I began to realize that the legal problem in this country is not just overlapping regulations, but also that the law has lost its touch with the people.

Our current legal language tends to be exclusive. Its words are rigid, its sound dry, and its logic often overrides the community's sense of justice. Amidst this situation, I see Javanese culture—with all its ethical heritage—as a bridge. It can teach that justice isn't just about who's right and who's wrong, but rather about who's willing to maintain harmony together.

The Javanese have a phrase "ngerti, ngrasa, lan nglakoni" (knowing, feeling, then carrying out). This is not only an attitude, but also a more humane approach to law. A law that not only judges but also understands.

However, the challenges are significant. When tradition is brought into the realm of formal law, misunderstandings often arise. Some view culture as a form of backwardness. In fact, it is precisely within culture that social systems that have been proven to sustain society for centuries.

I'm not saying we should completely return to customary law and abandon the modern legal system. No. But I believe the two can complement each other. The spirit of law can be revived if it is willing to listen to the whispers of its ancestors.

At the end of this chapter, I would like to invite readers to re-examine law not as something separate from our culture, but as part of it. Living law is not only what is written in statute books, but also what is rooted in the behavior and values of society.

And if we want to build a more just Indonesia, perhaps the first step is not to create new laws but to re-understand the laws that have long lived within ourselves.

Among the many noble values that have grown in Java, I've found one common thread that consistently emerges in conflict resolution: a willingness to exercise restraint. This is not weakness, but wisdom. In Javanese philosophy, there's a term called "ngalah untuk menang," which shouldn't be taken literally as surrender, but rather as a strategy for achieving greater victories—inner victory, social victory, and sometimes, spiritual victory.

When I studied law in college, I was taught about legal logic, the theory of justice, and the principle of legal certainty. But at home, I was taught that not all truths need to be spoken. There are times when silence is more reassuring. There are times when forgiveness is more educational than punishment.

Many outsiders assume that this culture makes Javanese people passive, uncritical, or afraid to speak out against injustice. In fact, it is precisely within this subtlety that great strength lies. The strength to remain sane in a harsh world. The strength to resolve conflicts without shedding blood or humiliating others.

I see this as having great potential for building a more civilized legal system. Not a law that merely judges and punishes, but a law that restores. One that reconciles. One that maintains social relations intact, even after the dispute has ended.

In my practice as an advocate, I strive to embody these values. In every case I handle, I not only ask who is right and who is wrong, but also who can open the way for dialogue. Who still has good intentions? Who can be consulted to resolve the problem without destroying each other.

As a citizen, I feel it's time for Indonesian law to have a more humane face. And we can find that face in the mirror of our own culture—including Javanese culture. From there, we learn that the law doesn't have to be frightening. It can protect. It can educate. It can be a bridge, not a chasm.

So, when I wrote this book, I wasn't comparing culture and law as two opposing entities. On the contrary, I was trying to show that the two can be integrated if we are willing to dig deeper into our roots.

And perhaps, that is where the soul of Indonesian law lies that we have been searching for: not in a pile of regulations, but in our conscience as a great, gentle nation, and one that dares to guard its dignity wisely.

As a lawyer who frequently appears in court, I'm accustomed to the courtroom atmosphere: formal, stiff, and stressful. But what truly resonates most with me isn't the debates before the panel of judges, but rather my encounters with people marginalized by the legal system itself—those who don't know where to turn, those who lose not because they're at fault, but because they lack access.

In the villages, I saw how strongly customary law is still enforced. This isn't because the residents are unfamiliar with the Civil Code or the Criminal Code, but because, for them, justice is something simpler: resolved through deliberation, culminating in mutual forgiveness, and then forgotten over a tumpeng (rice cone) and communal prayer. There's something deeply human about this that can't be found in any legal text.

Of course, formal law has an important place, especially in a modern state that must guarantee the equal protection of the rights of all citizens. But in a system that is increasingly technocratic, bureaucratic, and sometimes increasingly distant from our cultural roots, I feel the need to reconnect the roots of law with local wisdom. Not to replace it, but to enhance it.

As a writer, I try to capture this shift in my writing—that law isn't a singular entity that lives in a courtroom, but something that grows out of the way we talk, solve problems, and nurture relationships. I even wrote a song about it: "Justice isn't a loud voice, but a quiet embrace." Because in many places, people don't need to win; they just want to be understood.

We often forget that laws that are too rigid can lose their vitality. This is where culture comes into play—as a spirit that penetrates the rigid framework of formal law, lending tenderness to overly legalistic justice, and restoring humanity to the process of conflict resolution.

And perhaps most importantly: culture makes room for hope. It not only dictates what is and isn't permissible, but also shows that there is a path to healing, to reconciliation, to reconciliation without losing self-respect.

As a Javanese child, I feel a moral responsibility to convey this message: that local wisdom is not merely a legacy of the past, but the foundation for a more inclusive legal future. Because only by rediscovering who we are—from language, values, to philosophy of life—can we build a legal system that truly reflects the face of the nation.

And at the end of all this journey, I came to a simple but profound conclusion: that tracing the legal path in ancestral lands is not only about remembering the past, but also about finding a direction for the future—a direction that favors justice, humanity, and wisdom that have been growing since before this republic was founded.

I remember a story from my childhood, when a village elder resolved an inheritance dispute by simply sitting cross-legged, listening to all parties speak, and concluding with one short sentence: "The old man gives his consent, the young man gives his consent." It sounded so simple, it didn't even have any legal force in the context of modern law.

But strangely, everyone present complied. There was no more hostility. There was no need for court documents. And what remained was relief—justice felt, not just written.

In today's legal world, we often get caught up in procedures. We forget that the essence of justice is feeling. The feeling that someone is heard, respected, and considered a whole person. And that feeling cannot be created through rigid articles. It grows from cultural understanding, from a willingness to enter into the context of the lives of the people the law is supposed to protect.

This is what I mean by the spirit of Indonesian law—not a law that simply imitates the systems of other countries, but a law rooted in the very soil we stand on. A law that recognizes the voices of market women who lose their stalls, the voices of workers who fear being fired for speaking out, or the voices of farmers whose land is taken without them even understanding the documents they have signed.

I'm not saying that everything must be resolved through customary law. But formal law must learn to listen more. Learn from traditions that have been proven to maintain harmony for centuries, even before this nation existed. We can establish a strong judicial system without losing our human touch. We can establish firm rules without becoming rigid.

And as an advocate, I see this not as a challenge, but as an opportunity. An opportunity to form a generation of lawyers who are not only good at arguing in the courtroom, but also understand the way of speaking that people hear most: the language of the heart.

Tracing the legal legacy of my ancestors has led me to a new understanding that this profession is not merely a tool for seeking legal victory, but a bridge between justice and society. A path to reconnecting the law with the nation's conscience.

I believe that great law is law that grows from its own soil. And that soil, in the Indonesian context, is more than just geography. It is a legacy of values, language, music, perspectives, and ways of life. A law that embraces all of these will not only be respected, but will be remembered—not for its power, but for its wisdom.

And that is where I lay the first foundation of this book: on the realization that we are not building a completely new legal system, but rather reviving something that has long been embedded—the spirit of justice from our ancestral homeland.

With every step I take along the legal corridors of this country, I often discover that Indonesia is not just a republic of law, but a large house built on values, narratives, and conscience. In this house, law is not merely a text printed in the state gazette, but something that lives in the greetings of elders, the whispered prayers of mothers, the beats of gamelan music, and even in the silence of the common people awaiting justice.

As a lawyer, I've learned that the power of argument comes not only from logic, but also from empathy. As a writer, I realize that laws won't last if they aren't written with the soul of the nation in mind. And as a songwriter, I understand that the voice of justice must have a melody that resonates with everyone, from the village to the capital, from the common people to the rulers.

Therefore, this chapter is not closed, but laid—as a foundation. To fully understand Indonesian law, we cannot simply sit on campus or read jurisprudence. We must go to the roots, listen to the voice of the land, and read the law from the perspective of how this nation loves and improves itself.

Only by tracing the legal trail from our ancestral homeland can we understand that justice is not an end in itself — but rather a long journey toward wisdom, which we must continue to nurture together.

We will now go deeper—exploring the symbols, stories, and folk performances that have long held secrets about how this nation understands power, authority, and justice. We will enter the world of wayang, a world that not only entertains but also guides—through shadows that actually provide light.

In this diverse country, the law cannot operate alone. It must work hand in hand with culture. No law can be truly just if it doesn't understand the context of the society it serves. Indonesia, with its diverse customs and languages, teaches that justice is not just about winning or losing in court, but about feeling accepted and respected.

That's why, when I formally studied law, I also went back to my Javanese roots—and my Indonesian roots. I realized that many principles of customary law or ancestral teachings are actually more capable of resolving conflicts sustainably than decisions that win on paper but leave scars in the hearts of the people.

This chapter encourages us to embrace learning from local wisdom. Indonesian law doesn't have to be a perfect imitation of Western systems, as we possess equally valuable resources: mutual cooperation, deliberation, and respect for social balance. These values are not just a thing of the past. They are the foundation of the future.

As a lawyer, writer, and songwriter, I share the same mission in three different worlds: to speak up for justice. And that voice will be heard louder if it grows from one's own soil, from one's own folklore, from the soul of one's own nation.

In the following chapters, I will continue to explore how justice in the Indonesian context is not an abstraction — but something that is alive, flowing through culture, and can be recognized through various symbols and narratives.

Because true justice in this country must not only be fair according to the law, but must also feel fair in the hearts of its people.

The legal legacy of our ancestors' land is not just a story of articles and procedures, but a reflection of the nation's spirit, which continues to seek justice with feeling, not just rules. From the practices of indigenous communities to the dynamics of modern law, I learned that deeply rooted law will always find a way to become meaningful—not only legitimate in the eyes of the state, but also just in the eyes of conscience.

## CHAPTER 2
## Puppetry, Authority, and Discourse of Justice

Wayang is more than just an artistic performance. It is a collective reflection of Javanese society's understanding of power, morality, and justice. Behind a screen, a small stage emerges, presenting a battle between good and evil, between dharma and adharma, between power and wisdom. But what's remarkable is that wayang doesn't teach a black-and-white world—it teaches that every character, even the seemingly most holy, harbors doubts and failures. And it is from there that lessons about humane justice emerge.

As a lawyer, I see that the modern legal system is often trapped in rigid structures. But wayang teaches that justice must often be delivered with wisdom, not simply power. The authority of a wayang character, such as Semar or Arjuna, is born not from position, but from behavior and noble intentions. This is where the law finds its deeper breath—not only enforced, but also felt and accepted.

Wayang also conveys a philosophical message about the importance of maintaining balance. In every play, even when truth triumphs, that victory is always accompanied by introspection and an awareness of responsibility. This is a form of justice deeply rooted in culture—a justice that doesn't silence the enemy, but heals wounds.

In this chapter, I want to encourage readers to see that the concepts of authority and justice in Indonesia have long been alive in tradition, even long before the imposition of colonial law. And if we want to build a strong legal system, we must start by recognizing that cultural heritage like wayang is not just entertainment—but a worthy foundation for future legal inspiration.

Among the many characters in the world of wayang, Semar is the most paradoxical and at the same time the most philosophical. He is not a king, not a knight, not a figure with formal power, but instead he serves as the moral guide in the great stories. He has a funny face, a plump body, and simple movements—yet his words guide the direction of the story and the conscience of the main characters. Semar is a form of justice that doesn't strike, but reminds; doesn't punish, but advises. In the modern legal system, such a character is almost nonexistent—yet, he is much needed.

In everyday legal practice, we often encounter justice that is blunt at the top and sharp at the bottom. Someone can be severely punished for stealing food, while major corruptors can hide behind technical provisions and legal loopholes. This is where the lessons of wayang become relevant. Justice based solely on power is easily twisted. But justice born of moral authority, as portrayed by Semar, has far greater resilience. Authority does not mean fear, but rather respect for honesty and a commitment to the common people.

The figure of Arjuna, often portrayed as an ideal knight, is also imperfect. He often doubts, falters, and even makes mistakes. But his journey is one of maturity—he learns from every mistake, and that is what makes him a wise figure. This is a form of reflective justice: not one that always feels right, but one that is willing to grow and understand the context. Imagine if law enforcers in this country had a consciousness like Arjuna's: not believing that power is absolute, but continually questioning whether they have upheld justice completely.

Wayang doesn't stop at the realm of storytelling. It's present in the Javanese way of resolving problems: through discussion, sarcasm, and subtle, heartfelt language. In court, we too often see shouting, arguing, and even mutual humiliation. Yet, noble values like these—which have existed for hundreds of years—could be the salvation of our legal system, which is beginning to lose public trust.

This chapter does not aim to replace modern law with wayang. But I want to emphasize that law must not be blind to culture. In wayang plays, we discover that justice is not just an end in itself, but a long process that requires patience, wisdom, and respect from all parties.

And as long as the law is still considered to belong to the strong, the voice of the people will continue to be left behind.

In many wayang plays, we find that conflicts aren't always resolved through physical force or grand warfare. In fact, behind the battles between warriors, there are profound inner dialogues—about right and wrong, about intentions and consequences, about responsibility and sacrifice. Even in the legendary Baratayuda War, the Pandawa's victory wasn't simply a matter of who was stronger, but who was more prepared to bear the moral burden of their decisions.

This reminds us that justice is never free from values. And this is what the overly technocratic positive legal system often forgets: that every article has a context, every verdict has a social impact, and every gavel strike has an echo that can shake the lives of ordinary people. In Javanese society, a person is judged not only by outward actions, but also by "rasa" — an ethical concept that assesses refinement, sincerity of intention, and a willingness to take responsibility even when no one is watching.

A lawyer or judge who only masters positive law, without understanding the "sense of justice" of the society in which he or she works, will always be alienated in the public eye. He or she may be legally correct, but not necessarily culturally just. Therefore, establishing a down-to-earth legal system means absorbing the values of local wisdom into our ways of thinking and acting. We are not talking merely about customary law, but about the cultural spirit that can shape how people understand justice.

Wayang, with all its symbols and metaphors, is a rich laboratory for justice. In it, we can learn that justice does not mean treating everyone equally, but rather that everyone is given their rightful place according to their dignity. That the law cannot be rigidly standardized but must be flexible to respond to ever-changing social realities.

I believe the future of Indonesian law lies not in simply strengthening institutions or revising laws, but in our ability to explore the noble values of our own culture as a moral foundation. And in that regard, wayang is a heritage too precious to ignore.

One of the most profound aspects of Javanese culture is its tendency to convey truth through symbols, not shouting. Wayang is an art form that doesn't directly preach, but rather allows the audience to reflect. Within it, there are layers of messages that must be carefully unraveled—because in Javanese culture, wisdom isn't spoken aloud, but rather delivered quietly.

We can see how great wayang characters like Kresna don't always speak at length, but a single sentence can change the course of a story. He is a symbol of a leader who speaks with meaning, not volume. Similarly, in the legal world, a wise judge or lawyer isn't the most vocal, but one who is able to read the situation and weigh justice from various angles—including those not written in the law.

Wayang also teaches about roles and balance. Not everyone has to be a hero. Not every problem must be resolved with victory. There's a time to advance, and there's a time to retreat. In today's fast-paced and competitive world, these lessons can feel unfamiliar. However, resolving legal conflicts often requires patience, a willingness to reconcile, and respect for the process as part of justice itself.

The punakawan characters—Semar, Gareng, Petruk, and Bagong—are not merely story additions, but symbols of the strength of ordinary people. They represent critical voices, humorous voices, and even conscience in an overly serious world. If our courts are overly formal and underwhelmed by emotion, then the inspiration of the punakawan should serve as a reminder: the law must remain down-to-earth, friendly, and connected to real people, not simply follow the logic of texts.

And most importantly, wayang creates a shared space for expressing truth without clashing egos. It is a medium of compromise, contemplation, and transformation. In an era when our society is increasingly divided by binary narratives—black and white, right and wrong, pros and cons—wayang offers a third narrative: a dialogical narrative, which is the key to building a more humane justice.

When I first started my career as a lawyer, I often reflected on the wayang scenes I had witnessed as a child. Sitting in court, dealing with a troubled client, or having to decide on a legally sound but morally dubious strategy—I found that memories of characters like the honest Werkudara, the shrewd Kresna, or the wise Semar shaped my decision-making.

In fact, I once abandoned a certain legal action simply because I remembered a wayang saying: "Even a righteous person isn't necessarily righteous if their intention is to defeat." That sentence is simple, but it was enough to restrain me from taking actions that, while legally valid, could harm substantive justice and a sense of humanity.

Wayang taught me more than just about who wins and loses, but about how every decision carries spiritual and social responsibilities. And perhaps this is what has been missing from our legal system: a living and relevant ethical framework, not just written on paper. We too often enforce articles, but forget to uphold conscience. We are preoccupied with procedure, but forget about substance.

In the realm of advocacy, I've found that many conflicts can be resolved not by the strength of argument alone, but by the closeness of feeling between the disputing parties. This is precisely what is taught in wayang plays: conflict doesn't have to end in destruction; it can be transformed into a life lesson if handled with compassion and wisdom.

Therefore, when discussing legal reform in Indonesia, I feel we need to revisit the wayang stage. It is there that law, culture, and humanity come together in harmony. It is there that a leader's authority is tested not by title or power, but by their ability to position themselves in a just and equitable manner for all.

Wayang is not only a reflection of culture, but also a reflection of the inner workings of the law we should be striving for. In the shadows of the blencong swaying on the screen, we find a more subtle, deeper, and more humane narrative of justice—a justice that doesn't speak loudly, but touches the heart. As a lawyer who grew up in Java, I've learned that true justice doesn't always have to come from the judge's gavel, but can come through gentleness, through narrative, and through local wisdom passed down through generations. So, as long as we still have a living culture, as long as wayang is still performed and its values are lived, we still have hope: that the law in this country can be more than just a system—it can be a soul that protects, heals, and unites.

# CHAPTER 3
## Javanese Philosophy

If law is the body, then philosophy is its soul. For the Javanese, life is not simply a series of decisions, but an inner journey guided by values that existed long before the first laws were written. Javanese philosophy doesn't shout, it doesn't force, and it isn't black and white. It works in silence, in practice, in how one maintains a balance between the inner and the outer, between rights and obligations, between power and feeling.

Concepts such as "tepa selira" (empathy towards others), "nrimo ing pandum" (accepting with an open heart), "sumeleh" (surrendering but still trying), and "eling lan waspada" (always being aware and alert), are not motivational jargon, but rather life principles that shape the way Javanese people behave — including in dealing with conflict, power, and justice.

As a lawyer, I see these philosophies as not contradictory to modern law; instead, they can serve as a bridge between formal norms and local wisdom. For example, when someone chooses mediation over taking a dispute to court, it's not because they're weak, but because they uphold harmony—rukun agawe santosa, crah agawe bubrah. This is a more rooted, nuanced, and sustainable form of justice.

In practice, I often find that the most successful resolutions aren't those that force victory, but those that restore relationships between people. Javanese philosophy teaches that not everything must be resolved with force, and not all rights must be claimed to the fullest. There's wisdom in choosing when to advance, when to yield, and when to simply remain silent with sincerity.

In today's fast-paced modern world, Javanese values are often considered slow, even outdated. Yet, in their slowness, they harbor extraordinary reflective power. Philosophies like "alon-alon asal kelakon" (along with the law) are not merely an invitation to slow down, but a call to slow down in judgment and to act rashly—something highly relevant in legal practice.

As a lawyer, I often encounter clients who want everything fast: a quick win, a quick resolution, a quick recognition. But I know that not everything can be forced with instant logic. Some cases require time to calm emotions, reassess intentions, and build bridges between past wounds. In moments like these, I'm reminded of the concept of mikul dhuwur mendhem jero—lifting high the good in others and burying deep their bad. This is a form of justice that is not only legal, but also cultural.

Javanese philosophy also introduces us to the inner dimension of justice. In court, someone may win on paper. But does he also win in his heart? Does the decision bring peace, or does it sow new resentment that will one day explode? Javanese philosophy invites us to think not only linearly, but holistically—that law cannot be separated from feeling, and true victory is when all parties can return home with peace of mind.

I believe that Javanese philosophy can be the foundation for the future transformation of Indonesian law—not to replace the existing system, but to complement it. Because justice is not just about procedures and articles, but also about how we treat fellow human beings as brothers and sisters, as brothers in this journey of life.

One of the most profound philosophies in Javanese tradition is sangkan paraning dumadi—the awareness of the origin and purpose of human life. This philosophy teaches that every human being comes from the Creator and will return to Him. In a legal context, this understanding presents a very high moral awareness: that every decision, action, and intention will return to us—if not in a worldly court, then before our conscience or God.

This value shapes the Javanese way of viewing responsibility. Law is not merely a tool of power, but a reflection of inner responsibility. A wise leader fears not only violating state law but also violating the inner order believed to maintain the balance of the universe. That is why, in Javanese tradition, someone who is legally wrong but acts with sincere intentions is often respected. Meanwhile, those who win by cunning—even if legally valid—are considered to have lost their true dignity or honor.

Philosophies like sepi ing pamrih, rame ing gawe (not prioritizing personal interests, being diligent in work) are highly relevant to the legal profession. An ideal advocate is not one who pursues fame, but one who works quietly to uphold justice. In my practice, I often ask myself: am I working for fees, to win cases, or to help clients find peace? Javanese philosophy forces me to continually balance the professional with the spiritual, legal strategy with inner sincerity.

In the values of ajining diri ana ing lathi, ajining rogo ana ing pakaian—a person's self-respect lies in their speech, and their physical dignity lies in their attitude and appearance—we also see how Javanese culture places ethics as the foundation of honor. As a lawyer, my words can be a lifesaver or a ruin. Therefore, I have learned not to speak carelessly, not to be tempted by empty rhetoric, and to always uphold integrity in every legal argument I make.

Javanese philosophy is not only a cultural heritage, but also a foundation of character. It fosters a mentality of service, not of conquest. It instills humility amidst achievement, and reminds us that in life and law, what matters most is not who wins—but who remains true to the values of goodness until the very end.

Javanese philosophy is inseparable from natural symbols. Mountains, sea, wind, and fire—all reflect human character. Mountains symbolize steadfastness and patience; the sea represents broad-mindedness; wind represents flexibility; and fire represents passion and courage. For Javanese people, true justice exists when all these elements are in harmony. A just legal system is not only as strong as fire, but also as calming as the wind, as embracing as the sea, and as firm as a mountain.

This awareness of balance gives rise to tepa salira—the ability to put oneself in another's shoes. In the legal realm, this concept is crucial. A lawyer who understands tepa salira will not simply defend a client with blind fanaticism, but will also seek to understand how it impacts the opposing party, society, and even the client's own future. It serves as a reminder that empathy is not weakness, but rather the deepest form of justice.

There's also the value of nglurug tanpa bala, menang tanpa ngasorake—attacking without troops, winning without humiliating. This is an elegant form of victory, a victory that doesn't destroy. As a lawyer, I've learned that there are times when we don't need to humiliate our opponents; simply showing the truth is enough. Justice doesn't always have to come from a head-on confrontation; sometimes it comes through moral fortitude, consistent patience, and clear dialogue.

In the courtroom, I saw how quickly people could become violent. But in Javanese philosophy, violence is actually a form of inner imbalance. A truly strong person is one who can control themselves. This value made me realize that in my defense, I bring not only logic but also heart. I fight not only for legal certainty, but also for the integrity of the human soul.

In Javanese tradition, everything comes back to one point: urip iku mung mampir ngombe—life is just a stopover for a drink. Therefore, every role we play—as judge, lawyer, client, or ordinary citizen—is merely a brief passage on the journey to eternity. When we realize that all of this is fleeting, we will be more careful in our words, actions, and decisions. Javanese philosophy does not ask us to be perfect, but to be aware—and awareness itself is the beginning of true justice.

One of the pinnacles of Javanese philosophy lies in the principle of manunggaling kawula lan gusti—the union of servant and God. This philosophy asserts that in every human action, including upholding the law, there is always a spiritual dimension that must not be ignored. True justice, according to this philosophy, not only satisfies logic but also touches the conscience and aligns with divine values. Because behind every article, there is always a human being; and behind every human being, there is always the subtle yet real voice of God.

I'm reminded of the story of our Javanese ancestors who prioritized rembugan—deep, calm deliberation—in resolving disputes. They believed that within silence and wisdom, there is always a middle ground. This value inspires me that in many modern legal cases, a dialogical approach can be far more salutary than mere competition. This philosophy places justice not in the hands of the strongest, but in the clearest heart.

In addition, in Javanese life, there is a high respect for karma — cause and effect. What is planted today, will be reaped tomorrow. This principle indirectly encourages a restorative justice system, where every mistake is not only punished, but also directed towards recovery. This is what makes me even more convinced that legal reform in Indonesia needs to touch the roots of culture, not just change regulations. If we want to build a humane legal system, then philosophies such as karma, andhap asor, and tepa salira must not only be an oral legacy — but rather be used as a basis for policy formulation.

I didn't learn this knowledge in college, but rather through life—from sitting with elders, from listening to old songs, from contemplating my travels to villages where law and culture still go hand in hand. There, I discovered that Javanese philosophy isn't just a teaching, but a way of life. It guides not just how we think, but how we become human.

In the whirlpool of increasingly fast times, Javanese philosophy is often considered ancient or irrelevant. In fact, behind its softness, there is extraordinary resilience. He taught that strength does not always have to be shown with a loud voice or tensed muscles, but with steadfast calm, active patience, and clarity of heart in the face of injustice. These are the values I am trying to bring to the world of law—not to replace the existing system, but to root it more deeply in the ground we walk on.

I see how modern society often seeks justice in the form of instant victories. However, Javanese philosophy reminds us that justice is a long process that involves character development. A person who demands their rights must also be prepared to shoulder their responsibilities. A judge who renders a verdict must also be able to weigh not only the facts but also their impact on the social order and the spiritual well-being of the parties involved. This is a more comprehensive form of justice, as it involves not only the legal text but also the context of life.

As a lawyer, I'm often tasked with winning cases. But the further I've progressed, the more I've come to understand that the greatest victory comes when justice is understood by all parties—not just won by one. Javanese philosophy has been my guiding light, keeping me from losing my way amidst arguments, deadlines, and emotional pressure. It has given me a moral anchor: that the legal profession is not just a career path, but a lifelong pursuit, a devotion to balancing a world that is never truly balanced.

In the end, Javanese philosophy teaches that life and law both require balance. Life is not about winning alone, but about winning together. Principles such as sumeleh (surrender wisely), eling lan wari (remember and be alert), and ngeli ning ora keli (go with the flow without drifting) form a way of viewing conflict and its resolution in a more comprehensive way. For Javanese people, justice is not just a matter of who is right or wrong, but who is able to maintain harmony.

As a legal professional, I recognize that today's world lacks space for reflection. Everything is fast-paced, decisive, and final. However, from the philosophy of my ancestors, I've learned that hastily enacted laws may be valid, but they are not necessarily wise. It is at this point that the legacy of Javanese wisdom needs to be revived, not as a romanticization of the past, but as a strategy for the future. So that our laws don't lose their soul. So that our society doesn't lose its direction. And so that all of us, in small and large steps, continue to walk in the light of the values that guide us to become fully human.

In the daily lives of Javanese people, we see how the law isn't always presented in black and white. There's a gray area, and that space is where wisdom resides. When two people have a dispute, villagers don't immediately take the matter to court. They prioritize deliberation, seek a peaceful solution, listen to consciences, and even consider each party's social standing and feelings. In forums like village discussions, justice isn't measured by who wins, but by who can subdue their ego for the common good.

This value is invaluable in an increasingly technocratic and cold legal world. Because, behind the piles of documents and articles, we are talking about human beings—with wounds, hopes, and dignity. Javanese philosophy invites us to see all of this as an inseparable whole. The law must not uproot a person from their roots as a human being. It must be a bridge, not a sledgehammer.

When I defend a client, I bring more than just legal arguments to the courtroom. I also bring empathy, respect, and sometimes, prayer. Not because I'm a devout religious person, but because I know that in Javanese culture, success isn't just about hard work, but also about pure intentions and steps that are in harmony with the universe.

Javanese philosophy not only shapes our thinking but also guides our attitudes toward conflict, justice, and humanity. It teaches that law is not simply about right or wrong, but about maintaining harmony amidst life's imperfections. From values like rukun (harmony), tepa selira (community), and adigang-adigung-adiguna (community harmony), I learned that true justice doesn't have to scream to be heard. It exists in firm gentleness, in the courage not to retaliate, in decisions that favor balance, not just victory. And there I discovered that law and culture are never separate—they guide each other, measure each other, and together they keep the soul of the nation from losing its way.

# CHAPTER 4
## Javanese Songs as Testimonials

In Javanese culture, tembang (song) is more than just a song. It is an oral heritage containing values, messages, and even subtle yet incisive social criticism. Tembang teaches, reminds, and records. In a society where directly challenging those in power can be dangerous, tembang provides an alternative—gentle yet impactful, calm yet sharp. Therefore, it is no exaggeration to call Javanese tembang a testimony: the voice of the people, eternally recorded, expressing the truth in a form that is almost undeniable.

As a lawyer who also loves art, I see tembang as evidence that Javanese people have long expressed justice, sadness, and even dissatisfaction through beautiful yet meaningful lyrics. In the tembang Macapat, for example, we discover a life philosophy that shapes human character from childhood—from Pangkur, which teaches restraint, to Dhandhanggula, which speaks of beauty and hope. Behind the structure of its meter and rhythm, hidden silent voices record the times, remind those in power, and strengthen the hearts of ordinary people.

Some might view tembang as a form of entertainment or a past tradition worth remembering but no longer relevant. But I see it differently. Tembang embodies a Javanese way of understanding life, organizing one's inner self, and conveying social criticism without necessarily inciting open conflict. Tembang provides a space where the common people can speak without resorting to weapons; where concerns can be sung and, in doing so, conveyed to those in power without violating anyone's dignity.

Let's take the example of the Gambuh song, which is often performed in a setting of contemplation or advice. Its lyrics often speak of honesty, wisdom, and loyalty to noble life values. When people experience injustice or betrayal from their leaders, they don't always resort to physical resistance. They create songs. And within these songs, there's hidden criticism, subtle satire, and unwavering hope. This isn't a form of resignation, but a cultural strategy to maintain dignity while still conveying a message.

As a songwriter who also works in the legal field, I feel the power of song to touch areas beyond even legal arguments. It speaks directly to the heart. It transcends bureaucratic barriers, positive law, and even fear. In song, the voice of the people becomes eternal. It cannot be silenced, for it is embedded in culture. Even as legal texts change and systems evolve, the song lives on—a reminder that true justice must side with the voices often ignored.

In many villages across Java, especially during traditional ceremonies or important events such as weddings, funerals, and harvest festivals, tembang (Indonesian traditional songs) are still sung. Sometimes they are performed by female singers (sinden) accompanied by gamelan, sometimes by elders singing them on their verandas at dusk. This is not just a performance—it reinforces identity, imparts values, and reminds us of the direction of life. Behind these gentle songs are reflections on time, responsibility, and social justice.

Even seemingly personal or romantic songs often contain profound moral values. For example, the song "Asmaradana," which speaks of love and longing, often includes messages about loyalty, patience, and steadfastness amidst trials. All of this demonstrates that Javanese people never separate feeling from logic, law from the heart, and culture from everyday life.

If we as a nation want to build a law that is firmly rooted, we cannot rely solely on legal texts. We need to re-listen to the voices in songs—voices that may have been nearly forgotten, but which hold authentic local wisdom. Because a law that cannot speak the language of culture is a foreign law in its own country.

As a lawyer born and raised in Java, I believe that understanding tembang is one way to listen to the people. And in a world where the people's voices are often drowned out by the hustle and bustle of power, tembang continues to sing—quietly, but meaningfully. It is testimony. It is hope. It is a legacy of justice in melody.

Songs are not just voices of the past, but reflections of life that continue to resonate today. In the silence of rural nights, when electricity may be out and technology unreliable, songs become a means of intergenerational communication. They connect stories, pass on ethics, and reconnect beliefs to noble values. Each verse contains insights into social structures, power relations, and even the Javanese philosophy of life regarding the balance between humans, nature, and the divine.

Songs also contain a kind of "inner constitution" that regulates etiquette, gender relations, and even leadership ethics. Values such as ajining dhiri saka lathi (self-respect depends on words) or sura dira jayaningrat, lebur dening pangastuti (strength will be melted by gentleness) demonstrate how Javanese culture embeds ethical values in musical expression. These values are often more deeply ingrained in society than formal law, as they are conveyed in a touching and deeply rooted form.

As a modern songwriter who strives to incorporate social messages into lyrics, I've learned that a song's power lies not only in its melody, but also in its content. And when I explored Javanese songs, I discovered the origins of all that. That music is not just art, but a tool for social change. That the words of a song can become an unwritten law, upheld by the collective consciousness.

Javanese songs are proof that the people have their own way of expressing their demands for justice, even without having to speak in formal forums. Therefore, when we talk about law and culture, let's not forget songs. For there, the people's laws speak. Quietly, but not to be ignored.

In my observation as a lawyer, songs often hold a narrative more powerful than the legal text itself. A song can convey injustices unheard by those in power, the anxieties of the common people unrecorded in the news, or the silent hopes never included in official speeches. Herein lies its true power—a song is not just a song, but a living, ever-evolving social archive.

The lyrics of traditional songs, passed down through generations, have become a kind of collective memory of right and wrong. They lack formal courts, yet they nonetheless teach ethics and justice. Even in societies lacking legal literacy, traditional songs have become a kind of cultural code: regulating how children should respect their parents, how leaders should act wisely, and how society should maintain harmony.

I often ask myself: if our laws often fail to touch the conscience of the people, perhaps it's because they don't understand their language. And tembang is that language—a language that can embrace, not just regulate. It doesn't oppress with articles, but touches with feelings. It doesn't threaten with sanctions, but enlivens with values.

In my experience composing songs, I've tried to recapture that spirit. How to create songs that are not only pleasant to listen to, but also make listeners reflect, ask questions, and take action. Because, like Javanese songs, a true song is more than just entertainment—it's a gentle form of resistance, a lasting reminder, and an unwavering love for one's homeland.

On numerous occasions when I've performed my own songs advocating for justice, I've often felt the same resonance as Javanese songs. There's an emotional resonance that's hard to describe, as if words sung from the heart can penetrate the walls of social indifference. Songs teach me that justice doesn't always have to be loud, nor does it have to be wrapped in rigid legal rhetoric. It can come through a soft voice, which is even more profound because it touches from within.

I'm reminded of the singers who sang meaningful songs during all-night wayang performances. Even though the audience came and went, their voices remained consistent, conveying their moral messages selflessly. They didn't need the spotlight or public recognition, because their mission was to convey values, not to seek applause. From them, I learned that striving for values through art is a long, lonely, but noble task.

And that's where the song finds its legal relevance. It serves as a witness to the times, a companion to the people, and a voice for a sense of justice that hasn't been written down in the pages of the law. Therefore, when we talk about living and impartial law, Javanese song has already demonstrated this.

Ultimately, Javanese tembang is more than just an artistic legacy—it is a spiritual testimony passed down through generations about how a nation understands justice, suffering, and hope. In the silence of the tembang's voice, lies a cry never uttered in court, but truly echoing in the hearts of the people. That's where I believe: if the law is to be truly just and down-to-earth, it must learn from the tones that grow from the soil, from words not written by officials, but sung by the people. Tembang is a reminder that eternal justice is not just what is recorded, but what is felt—and no law is stronger than the justice that lives in the soul of a nation.

Now, as society enters a fast-paced digital era, Javanese songs face the challenge of remaining relevant amidst a more bombastic and instant global music scene. Yet, amidst the noise of the times, the quiet voice of these songs feels increasingly important. Songs don't need to shout; they simply need to be heard with the heart. This is why I—as a lawyer and songwriter—feel compelled to bridge this heritage with today's world.

Through the music I create, I try to incorporate the values of Javanese tembang, not just in the melody or structure of the song, but in its spirit: giving voice to the silent, defending the vulnerable, and exposing often-hidden social wounds. In the courtroom, I speak through articles; on stage, I speak through lyrics. But both share the same goal: fighting for justice.

So, for me, tembang is not a relic of the past. It is a timeless moral guide. It is a way to heal a wounded society, strengthen a trembling heart, and remind us that justice is achieved not only through logic, but also through feeling. And as long as there are those who are willing to listen, tembang will live on—not just as art, but as the voice of the nation's conscience.

In my observation as an advocate, the greatest gap between the law and the people often lies not in the lack of rules, but rather in the distance of legal language from the public's cultural awareness. This is where tembang plays a crucial role. It teaches values without being patronizing, touches on morals without being overbearing, and shapes public opinion in a gentler yet profound way.

We can see examples of this in the songs taught to Javanese children from an early age—lullabies that subtly instill the values of honesty, patience, and self-control. This isn't just character education; it's legal education in its earliest and most fundamental form. Children are taught that every action has consequences, that life should be lived in harmony, and that others have rights that must be respected.

Songs taught social structure and a sense of responsibility, even before society knew the terms "constitution" or "human rights." When adults rehearse these old songs, they evoke not only nostalgia but also the realization that this wisdom has long been taught. Justice is not merely a judge's decision, but a life attitude that must be cultivated from an early age.

I believe that to build a strong legal society, we cannot rely on a repressive approach or simply reforming laws. We need a cultural approach. And tembang (song) is one of the most subtle yet powerful cultural weapons. It not only touches the ear but also carves meaning into the soul.

Javanese tembang is a witness that never dies. It holds wounds, hopes, criticism, and wisdom in a simple yet moving string of notes. In its silence, it teaches us that justice is not merely about punishing or justifying, but also about understanding, remembering, and forgiving. As a lawyer immersed in culture, I have learned that tembang is not only a means of expression, but also a reminder: that noble law is born from a gentle heart, from a mind willing to listen to the quietest whispers of the voiceless people. And perhaps, before the articles can speak, tembang has already testified.

Now, as we move into the next chapter, we will explore further the source of that inner voice: the Javanese philosophy that shapes the nation's framework of thought, attitude to life, and moral direction—a silent but solid foundation where law and culture intertwine.

# CHAPTER 5
## Village, the Scattered Puppeteer

If the city is the stage for modernization, then the village is the original script, often forgotten by its directors. As a lawyer who grew up in a rural landscape and now works amidst the roar of formal law, I witness a profound irony: that the village—once the lifeblood of customary and social law—is now largely excluded from the narrative of national legal development.

In my mind, a village is like an old puppeteer who's no longer involved in a wayang performance. He still adheres to the rules, still knows the plot, still possesses the wisdom to save the play from destruction. But his voice is starting to fade, and he's sometimes even considered obsolete. Yet, if we look deeper, a village isn't just a place to live; it's a place where law finds its meaning. It's there that deliberations are held without bureaucracy, and it's there that justice is meted out through mutual cooperation, not through mutual demands.

However, globalization and formal legal systems are not always friendly to villages. Many decisions are made without involving those who live closest to the land, nature, and traditions. When laws are passed without their voices, the law becomes foreign even in its own homeland.

Villages should not be simply objects of development or targets of legal aid. They are subjects, even puppeteers, capable of re-weaving social relations in ways no court can. In every traditional ceremony, in the rhythm of the planting season, in the way they resolve disputes without violence—principles of justice, perhaps unwritten, yet alive, are hidden.

This is where I rediscovered my roots: that to build just laws, we must not leave the village. Instead, we must return there, listening to the voices that have long been hidden in the silence of the fields, in the beating of the gong, in the advice of the elders who are now starting to be abandoned.

As I began delving into legal cases involving rural communities, I noticed a recurring pattern: they often fell victim to a lack of representation and regulatory complexity. Not because they didn't understand the law, but because the laws they received often forgot how to speak the language of the people.

An old farmer on the slopes of Mount Merapi once said to me: "Mr. Ari, the law comes like heavy rain—everyone gets wet, but there's nothing to drink." That phrase, though simple, captures the feelings of those who see state law come with complicated documents, threats of articles, and procedures that actually make them afraid to speak out.

Villages have their own systems. In many places, dispute resolution is carried out through deliberation forums that last late into the night. There are no judges, no power of attorney. But their decisions are obeyed and respected, even more so than court decisions. Why? Because justice in villages is not built on fear, but on shame, respect, and a collective awareness of maintaining harmony.

When a child steals a chicken, he isn't immediately imprisoned. He is summoned, discussed with the elders, and even invited to do community service as a form of restitution and reparation. This isn't a way of avoiding the law, but rather a form of restorative justice that grew out of cultural awareness—long before the term was used in modern legal systems.

Unfortunately, villages are increasingly being marginalized from their own capacities. Many village heads are losing their social authority, forced to submit to administrative structures that often don't understand the local context. Customary institutions are being marginalized, and villages are slowly becoming mere bystanders in a legal drama played out by outsiders.

As a lawyer who believes in down-to-earth law, I see the need for a reimagined approach. Villages don't need pity or mere assistance; they need to be engaged as equal partners. A just law is one that allows people to sit cross-legged in a joglo house, not merely stand proudly in an air-conditioned courtroom.

However, efforts to re-establish the role of villages as the axis of national values and morals cannot rely solely on nostalgia. They require concrete recognition within our legal system. Villages are more than just administrative areas; they are hubs of wisdom that have long been social puppeteers—controlling the narrative of life with their own puppets: community leaders, traditional elders, and once-respected informal institutions.

We must honestly admit: many agrarian disputes, customary land conflicts, and mining and development permit issues arise not simply because the law is absent, but because the law comes without listening. In Javanese tradition, a good puppeteer is one who can listen to the emotions of his audience, not just act out a story according to a script. So if villages are now the neglected puppeteers, it's because the larger system is reluctant to give space to storytelling from the stage.

As an advocate, I've seen that justice isn't just built in the Constitutional Court or high courtrooms. It's also formed in village halls, in simple pavilions where people gather to talk heart to heart. When village officials, traditional leaders, and residents sit together in a spirit of mutual cooperation, the resulting decisions are often more humane and binding than rigid formal legal rulings.

Ironically, these local "puppeteers" are increasingly losing their wayang (shadow puppeteers). Many of them are being pushed aside by context-blind modernization. Laws change, but grassroots voices remain muted. Not because they are mute, but because we no longer give them a platform.

I once attended a traditional court in a remote village in East Java. The issue was simple: a land boundary between two families. But what was interesting wasn't the substance of the dispute, but the process of resolving it. There were no microphones, no togas, no oaths taken under a holy book. All there was was a long wooden table, a few rattan chairs, and a cup of warm tea. The elders spoke slowly, giving each other space, listening to each other.

One thing I learned from that experience is that justice doesn't always come through power, but rather through trust. Villagers trust their elders because of their track record, their closeness, and their wisdom, formed not in academic settings, but in daily, dedicated service. This is a relational form of justice—rooted in values, not just rules.

Unfortunately, our legal system often focuses too much on legality, neglecting social legitimacy. Many legal decisions are procedurally valid, but fail to address the public's sense of justice. This is where strengthening the synergy between formal law and local wisdom becomes crucial. This is not meant to replace one with the other, but rather to bridge the gap between the two.

For me, the village is a place of endless learning. There, the law isn't just about articles, but about behavior. It's not just about winning or losing, but about healing and mutual understanding. When a troublemaking youth is asked to plant a tree as reparation, or when families at odds are invited to share a meal together at a feast—that's law in its most down-to-earth, and perhaps most sublime, form.

Many villagers now feel alienated in their own land. The arrival of large investors, infrastructure projects, and tourism expansion often alters the social landscape of villages without the consent of those directly affected. Local puppeteers—traditional leaders, spokespeople for the village's noble values—are marginalized by modern legal mechanisms, often imposed from outside, complete with technical language they cannot understand.

In my opinion, it's not just the legal system that needs to be grounded, but also how we understand justice itself. Villages are never just places; they are living spaces, where memories and identities are formed. When we craft laws without incorporating local elements, we're like writing a story without knowing the main character. And unfortunately, that main character is written off the stage of history.

We need a legal approach that isn't solely vertical, always looking from the center to the periphery. We need a horizontal way of thinking—recognizing that knowledge and policies can emerge from the people themselves. Customary law is not an outdated system, but rather one that has stood the test of time. It is flexible, contextual, and constantly negotiating with the values of its people.

Many villages in Indonesia, particularly in Java, still maintain the spirit of deliberation, mutual consultation, and tolerance. These values should not only be respected but also serve as inspiration for national legal reform. When villages lose their power as guardians of values, cities will also lose their source of morality.

I was once asked to assist in an inheritance dispute in a highland village. The disputing parties initially intended to take the case to the district court. However, before the trial began, a village elder said quietly but firmly, "If you win in court, you might get the house. But if you settle here, you can get your family back."

That sentence resonated. As a lawyer, I'm accustomed to evidence and articles. But as a human being, I can't deny that true justice often takes the form of restoring relationships, not punishment.

In the many cases I've handled in villages, I've come to realize one important thing: justice isn't an end in itself, but a way of life. In villages, conflict resolution isn't about winning or losing, but about restoring balance. In fact, if necessary, people are willing to "give in," not out of fear of losing, but because they realize that giving in can open the way back home.

This contrasts with the modern legal system, which almost always pits parties against each other—plaintiff versus defendant, plaintiff versus defendant. Yet, village communities teach that two parties may have different positions, but they still share one family, one village, and one history. If we underestimate this perspective, the law can become a dividing tool that actually damages the nation's social fabric.

Too often, we perceive villages merely as objects of development—passive entities to be organized, built, and "directed." But in reality, villages are centers of civilization with their own narratives. It is there that laws, customs, and values are enforced not by state mandate, but by collective consciousness. It recognizes not articles, but feelings.

As I delved into village life, I discovered that the true puppeteers were those who no longer occupied the stage. They weren't the figures spotlighted by cameras or mentioned in academic research. They were the mothers who preserved oral traditions, the fathers who decided family matters through nightly deliberations, and the young men who defended their village's rights despite not understanding the language of the law. They weren't law graduates, but they understood what justice was.

Unfortunately, many national policies fail to recognize this richness. Even the Village Law, while intended to provide space for village autonomy, is often implemented in a bureaucratic, rigid, and top-down manner. In fact, villages should be given the space to lead themselves—to become legal subjects, not merely objects of development. In many cases, villages don't need "help," they just need respect.

As a lawyer, I've learned that the law's job isn't to create uniformity, but to nurture diversity. And the village—in all its humility—is a reminder that true justice isn't born in an ivory tower, but in a barn that selflessly feeds its people.

There's an irony I can't ignore every time I return to the villages where I grew up and studied: the once-respected puppeteers have now lost their place on the stage. Not because they've lost their skills, but because our attention has shifted—from the slow, deep voices of wisdom to the fast, shallow voices of commotion. Those who once served as the keepers of stories and moral compasses are now merely the backdrop for hasty development.

Amidst the euphoria of modernization, the state often comes with promises of legality, without first considering the laws that have long existed in villages. Yet, villages are not empty spaces. They possess an ecosystem of values, relationships, and social logic no less complex than modern justice systems. In villages, conflicts are resolved not only through formal logic, but through an awareness of blood ties, history, and dignity.

I once witnessed a village head resolve a dispute between two families over a farm boundary. He didn't speak at length, didn't bring maps or documents. He simply summoned the elders, listened to both sides, and then said, "What's the point of winning the land if we can't shake hands tomorrow on Eid?" And the dispute was resolved. Not because the law was upheld, but because consciences were restored to their proper place.

This is where I feel the village holds the answers we've long sought. Amidst the hustle and bustle of the judiciary, amidst development figures and legal jargon, the village offers a space for contemplation: that true justice lies in harmony, not just judgment.

In the wayang tradition, the puppeteer is not just the storyteller—he is the interpreter of meaning. He determines who speaks, who remains silent, and when the truth emerges. So, when the village puppeteers are no longer heard, we have truly lost the tools to interpret our own lives. We pull up roots while hoping the tree grows taller.

When I spoke with an old puppeteer in a remote part of Central Java, he said calmly, "Nowadays, many people want to be king, but no one wants to sit and listen all night." It was a simple sentence, but it resonated with me as a lawyer. In the legal world, we are accustomed to speaking, arguing, and proving. But in the village, sometimes justice comes precisely because we remain silent and listen.

Today, village puppeteers have indeed been left behind. They are no longer invited to strategic spaces. But that doesn't mean they've disappeared. They remain, in the way communities make decisions, in the way young people ask questions, in the way farmers approach nature. If we want law in Indonesia to stand on its own ground, then we must bring them back to the forefront.

Not for romanticism. But because the village is a mirror: it shows us that living justice requires no strings attached, only one courage—to listen with the heart and appreciate what is no longer mentioned.

But in reality, the disappearance of puppeteers is not only a symbol of the loss of tradition—but a sign that our value system is experiencing disorientation. In village logic, puppeteers are more than just artists; they hold the space for interpretation, guide direction, and sometimes even mediate disputes. They know that what appears is not always true, and that truth requires space for reflection, not imposition.

As a lawyer, I've learned that justice applied without local wisdom often only adds to the pain. Modern law may have sophisticated instruments and a standard framework, but without listening to local rhythms, it's like a gamelan without a drum—without a tempo, without feeling.

The village and its puppeteers teach that justice is not just about winning or losing, right or wrong, but about maintaining relationships and preserving human dignity. For them, resolving conflict doesn't mean defeating an opponent, but rather avoiding division. Herein lies a crucial lesson: that a legal system that wants to take root must be willing to bend—to learn from the soil from which it grows.

And if the puppeteer is the guardian of harmony in the story, then the village is the stage where the story of this nation continues to be played out. We just need to be humble enough to listen to their narratives again.

# CHAPTER 6

## When the Courts Are No Longer Trusted

In every civilization, the courts are established as the supreme symbol of justice. They are expected to be the final refuge when all other hopes are dashed. However, what happens when this institution becomes a space of suspicion, doubt, and even abandonment?

In the various areas I visit, from cities to remote villages, there's one pattern I'm hearing more and more frequently: people avoiding the courts. Not because they don't want justice served, but because they no longer believe they're the place where justice can be found. Lengthy processes, high costs, and decisions that disfavor the weak—all of these are a pile of excuses that slowly build a wall of distrust.

They prefer to resolve conflicts through customary law, through deliberation, or even leave matters unresolved rather than confront a system that feels foreign and intimidating. And in many cases, that fear isn't just perception—it stems from real-life experiences: from bought witnesses, from bizarre demands, from judges who are no longer neutral, from cases that can be exchanged for power.

As a lawyer, I've never been anti-system. But I also can't turn a blind eye when the system we protect actually harms those who need it most. I believe true legal reform doesn't begin with building new courthouses or changing the color of togas. It must begin with the courage to recognize that public trust is the foundation of the law. Without it, all procedures are simply meaningless legal theater.

And when people no longer come to court, we should ask: who has really failed?

History records that modern courts were introduced to Indonesia with the promise of universal justice. However, in practice, this system often clashes with local values and does not fully accommodate the justice that exists within the community. In many places, especially outside the centers of power, courts appear as distant and inaccessible instruments of the state.

In the Javanese context, for example, traditional communities prefer village councils, elders, or even spiritual figures as the primary forum for resolving disputes. This is not solely due to the difficulty of accessing the courts, but rather because they find a more conscientious sense of justice in these informal systems. There are no intimidating formalities, no unfamiliarity with rigid legal language. Instead, there is a dialogical approach, prioritizing harmony and social integrity over mere retaliation.

Ironically, when society begins to return to these non-judicial solutions, the state often views them with suspicion. Yet, it is precisely there that lies the local wisdom that can serve as the foundation for our legal reform. Shouldn't law be born from the needs and experiences of society, not simply from voluminous books or articles written far from reality?

As a lawyer, I'm not calling for the abandonment of the courts. I'm calling for their restoration. Reviving public trust isn't enough with integrity campaigns or neutrality slogans. We need transparency that goes to the root. We need judges who not only master the law but also understand the social psyche of society. We need prosecutors who don't just pursue charges but seek substantive justice. And we need advocates who not only defend their clients but also uphold the values of the law itself.

The crisis of confidence in the judiciary is not the end of the world. It is an important signal that must not be ignored. It calls on all of us—law enforcement, academics, civil society, and even artists and cultural figures—to participate in reimagining how we understand and uphold justice.

Because if trust is the foundation, then our task is not simply to keep the court standing, but to ensure that it remains meaningful in the hearts of its people.

In everyday practice, we often encounter cases that are legally resolved, but socially, they actually cause deeper wounds. Families are torn apart by judges' decisions that disregard family values; indigenous communities are disturbed by a verdict that fails to understand the context of their ancestral lands. Herein lies the great irony of modern law, which is too preoccupied with defending procedural truth to ignore substantive justice.

Many judges decide cases without ever being psychologically present in the courtroom—playing their roles as mere operators of articles, not guardians of the nation's conscience. Likewise, justice seekers sitting as defendants or plaintiffs often feel alienated, anxious, and as if they are speaking in a language they don't understand.

As an advocate who has worked in courtrooms for many years, I've witnessed how the word "verdict" has become the end of a battle, but not always the end of a sense of injustice. This is where I learned that justice is never enough to simply put the guilty in jail or win the right on paper. True justice is when people feel treated as whole people—heard, understood, and respected.

The judiciary must not close itself off from criticism. Instead, it must open up space for dialogue and reform. Because if justice is no longer found there, the public will seek alternatives. They may return to more down-to-earth, informal forums, or fall into complete distrust of the entire state system. And that is more dangerous than simply losing legal legitimacy—it can divide the nation.

This chapter is not written to weaken the judicial institution. Rather, it is a call to strengthen it from within. By grounding the law, recognizing local values, and humanizing the justice process, we pave the way for a court that is respected not only for its authority but also trusted for its wisdom.

Distrust in the courts is not just a legal technicality—it is a social phenomenon that reflects the state's failure to deliver justice that is felt, not merely claimed. When a mother who loses a child due to medical negligence finds her civil suit unsuccessful due to a lack of formal evidence, or when a small farmer loses against a large corporation even though the entire village knows who was right, the narrative embedded in the public mind is no longer that "the law is upheld," but rather that "truth is for sale."

Moreover, this distrust can develop into collective trauma. People who feel betrayed by the system will withdraw from the legal process. They become apathetic, cynical, and even form groups that organize their own version of justice. This is a dangerous point—when official law loses its meaning in the eyes of the people, what will emerge is a "street court" that operates without ethical or procedural foundations.

As a lawyer, I've seen this frustration manifest. A client of mine once said, "I don't need to win, I just need my voice to be heard." It's a simple statement, but it conveys something profound: that in a court of law that has lost its sensitivity, people no longer expect justice, but merely validation of their suffering.

This poses a major challenge for all legal practitioners. Not just judges, prosecutors, and lawyers—but all elements of the system. It's time for the courts to be safeguarded not only for procedural integrity, but also for them to be built on a humanistic and cultural approach. Courtrooms must once again become places that listen, not just those that judge.

So the question is no longer: can the courts be trusted? But: what must we do together to restore trust in the courts?

When justice is no longer entrusted to the courtroom, it seeks its own path outside the system. This phenomenon is evident in the wave of digital activism, where people use social media as an "alternative courtroom." They voice their case, share videos, use hashtags, and hope that virality can replace the judge's gavel. This phenomenon is known as trial by public, and in some cases, it has succeeded in reopening investigations, but in many cases, it has also led to premature judgments.

This phenomenon implies something important: the human need to feel heard and defended cannot be delayed or silenced by bureaucratic complexity. A legal system that is slow, elitist, or opaque will be defeated by the mechanisms of a society hungry for swift justice. This can be interpreted as a call for change—not only in the structure of the courts, but also in the way law enforcement operates and thinks.

As a lawyer, I see the importance of building a narrative that the law belongs not to a handful of legal elites, but to the people. Therefore, the judicial process must be simplified without sacrificing integrity. Judges' decisions must be written in language the public can understand, and courtrooms must be open to public scrutiny without becoming spectacles.

In the Indonesian context, local wisdom such as deliberation, customary mediation, and restorative justice principles can be re-embraced as part of a more inclusive justice system. We don't have to always imitate Western systems in their formalistic forms. This nation has roots in conflict resolution that focuses on restoration, not just punishment.

The challenge going forward is not how the law is enforced through violence, but how the law is maintained so that it remains trusted. Because trust is not the result of decisions, but the result of repeated experience: that when someone knocks on the door of justice, the door is truly opened, not left closed by power, money, or rigid procedures.

# CHAPTER 7
## Customary Law: A Still Neglected Heritage

Among the hundreds of ethnic groups living in Indonesia, customary law is a constant breath, though often unheard. It isn't shouted on television, written in official state gazettes, and studied in depth in law schools. Yet customary law persists—memorized by elders, practiced silently by indigenous communities, and serving as an invisible foundation in the daily lives of millions of Indonesians.

Customary law is not simply a collection of ancient norms. It is the result of a dialectic between humans and their environment, between history and hope. In customary law, justice is not simply a matter of right and wrong, but how social harmony is restored. Herein lies its uniqueness: customary law prioritizes peace over victory.

Unfortunately, this heritage remains marginalized within the national legal system. Many judges ignore it because it's considered unofficial. Many lawyers don't understand it because they haven't been taught it. And many policies don't consider it because they're seen as hindering development. Yet, when national law fails to reach remote areas or when state courts lack trust, customary law remains alive and well.

In this chapter, I invite readers to examine more deeply how customary law, with all its richness and limitations, can actually serve as a source of inspiration for national legal reform. We will explore stories from various regions—from Bali, Sumatra, Kalimantan, to Papua—about how communities uphold values, organize their lives, and resolve disputes in their own ways.

Because perhaps, amidst the failure of modern law to answer the challenges of the times, the best answer has long been living with us—in the form of law born from the land of Indonesia itself.

One of the strengths of customary law lies in its communal approach. In this system, violations are not just individual matters, but also a breach of social balance. A violator of customary law is responsible not only to the victim but also to the community, whose relationships among members are disturbed. This is why dispute resolution under customary law often culminates in deliberation, restitution practices, or restoration rituals. All of these are aimed not at punishment, but at healing.

I once witnessed how, in a traditional Balinese village, a case of petty theft was not taken to the police station but resolved through a community forum. The perpetrator was brought in, not to be humiliated, but to be reminded of his position and role in village harmony. He was given social duties as a form of moral responsibility, and the victim was given customary compensation. All of this took place with emotional involvement, not merely procedural considerations.

However, precisely because it is unwritten and highly contextual, customary law is often considered unaccountable nationally. Yet, even national law is subject to interpretation and social context. Fear of customary law is often rooted more in central government arrogance toward the regions than in the substance of the law itself.

Even more distressing is how customary law is often undermined in land and resource disputes. Indigenous communities lose their customary rights because the state doesn't recognize their ownership system. Simply because they lack a certificate, land they've inhabited for hundreds of years can be taken by corporations with "legal standing." Here we see a profound paradox: formal law, supposedly guaranteeing justice, has become a tool of oppression, while customary law, which safeguards local sustainability and justice, is instead branded as antiquated.

It's time for Indonesia to reaffirm the position of customary law, not merely as a legacy, but as a living part of the national legal system. Customary courts must be given constitutional space. Law enforcement officers must be trained in local law. And indigenous communities must be given equal standing as guardians of the morals and laws that emerge from their own land.

Through this chapter, I want to open a conversation about how we can build an inclusive legal system that not only respects diversity but also empowers it as the nation's legal strength. Because if Indonesia wants to stand firmly as a nation of law, it must be based on its entire territory, not just the courthouses in the capital.

The problems that arise are not only at the formal or institutional level, but also in our perspective on the meaning of law itself. In the Western legal system we have adopted, law tends to be separated from the spiritual and cultural values of society. Law becomes a neutral and objective entity—yet in many indigenous communities in Indonesia, law is part of the belief system, the narrative about the world, and the relationship between humans and nature and their ancestors.

Take customary law in Papua, for example. There, law is not just rules, but also stories. Violations are not mere actions, but betrayals of the cosmic order. The process of reparation is not always rational within the logic of state law, but contains extraordinary symbolic and emotional depth. Unfortunately, these issues are often overlooked by the rigid and standardized national legal system.

We can also see how some indigenous communities in Kalimantan still practice the "pelikat kayu" (wood splitting system)—a traditional form of mediation that considers interfamily balance, social reputation, and the common good. This mechanism is often more effective and more acceptable than formal judicial verdicts, as it upholds the sense of justice inherent in the community.

However, the neglect of customary law also reflects a neglect of this nation's cultural identity. When young people are no longer taught their customs, when the next generation is more familiar with the Criminal Code than with rimbang law or local customary sanctions, what we face is not just a legal crisis, but a crisis of identity.

As a lawyer who also studies history and culture, I believe that we must not allow customary law to be marginalized as mere folklore. It is a living legal resource—rooted, contextual, and full of local wisdom. It is not meant to replace national law, but to complement it, balance it, and—in many cases—heal wounds that formal law cannot reach.

Upholding customary law is not a step back into the past, but rather a step forward towards a more relevant, more down-to-earth, and more humane justice.

If Indonesia wants to be known worldwide not only as a nation based on law, but as a just and wise nation, there's no other way: customary law must be recognized, respected, and empowered. Not merely respected in the letter of the law, but also enshrined in every dispute, in every village, and in every voice of the common people who have been neglected.

Efforts to revitalize customary law are not sufficient with administrative recognition alone. While many regions have Regional Regulations recognizing the existence of customary communities and their legal practices, very few actually involve the communities themselves in the formulation, implementation, and protection of these laws. As a result, customary law remains marginalized, often serving as a mere complement or symbol within the national legal system.

Another obstacle stems from the disparity in legal education. Many law enforcers—judges, prosecutors, and police—lack a thorough understanding of the diversity of customary law in Indonesia. They are trained in a uniform formal legal paradigm, which prioritizes written norms and procedural evidence. Therefore, when they encounter cases involving customary law, they often experience conflict rather than understanding. Customary law is considered insufficiently strong, insufficiently logical, or even insufficiently important to be considered in the judicial process.

In fact, in some cases, customary law has been able to resolve conflicts that formal systems have failed to resolve. For example, in East Nusa Tenggara, many cases of intergroup violence have been resolved through customary dowry (belis adat) or mediation by elders, which not only impose sanctions but also heal social wounds between the conflicting parties.

If we truly want an Indonesian legal system that reflects the true face of this nation, we must stop treating customary law as an inferior system. It is not a remnant of the past, but rather another form of legal civilization. In many ways, customary law is the most humane expression of justice—because it views perpetrators not simply as victims, but as part of a social network capable of restoration.

The challenge ahead is to build a bridge between state law and customary law. This requires not making one subservient to the other, but rather creating a mutually reinforcing harmony. A hybrid legal system that allows space for local wisdom while guaranteeing legal certainty nationally. This requires political courage, cultural sensitivity, and a commitment to law that sides with the people.

In closing this chapter, I want to emphasize that the future of Indonesian law cannot be built solely on the capital's tall buildings or imported law textbooks. It must grow from the roots, from the very soil we walk on, from a heritage we have nearly forgotten. Customary law is not a nostalgic romanticism, but rather a real potential to deliver living, grounded, and healing justice. If we still have a conscience as a nation, it is time to not only remember this legacy but also revive it.

In the daily lives of indigenous communities, law is not simply a set of rules, but a manifestation of collective values and wisdom. It lives on in the form of taboos, advice, rituals, and even deliberations involving all stakeholders. Customary law not only resolves conflicts but also prevents them in a way that procedural and impersonal state law cannot replace. Herein lies the power of customary law—it is integrated with everyday life.

However, precisely because of its fluid and contextual nature, customary law is often considered incompatible with a rigid, written national legal system. This is the main paradox that makes it difficult for customary law to find its proper place: it is too flexible for a rigid system, and too organic for bureaucratic logic.

Instead of embracing it, the state often attempts to regulate customary law through a formalization approach—recording, standardizing, and even forcing it into the mold of state law. However, this approach actually undermines the essence of customary law. The strength of customary law lies in its flexibility in understanding social contexts and changing times. Standardizing customary law is tantamount to freezing it.

What is needed is not uniformity, but authentic recognition. The state needs to create a space for dialogue between customary law and state law, not allow one to dominate the other. Judges must be given the freedom, even encouraged, to consider customary law as a legitimate source of law. Law universities must create space for in-depth study of legal pluralism, not simply relegating it to a final-semester sub-chapter.

Moreover, it's also crucial to build bridges between generations. Many indigenous youth are beginning to be uprooted from their cultural roots, no longer familiar with customary law, as it's considered outdated. This is where our role as writers, educators, and advocates comes in—reviving pride in our ancestral legal heritage, not as empty romanticization, but as a concrete tool for achieving social justice.

As a lawyer raised amidst the shifting values between modernity and tradition, I believe one thing: the future of Indonesian law lies not only in legislative reform, but also in reconciliation with our own cultural identity. And customary law, if given the space it deserves, can serve as both a moral foundation and an ethical bridge in our navigating national legal system.

One of the greatest challenges to preserving customary law is the fragmentation and inconsistency in its legal recognition. The 1945

Constitution does recognize the existence of customary law communities as long as they are alive and in keeping with current developments. However, this phrase has become a double-edged sword. On the one hand, it opens the door to legality, but on the other, it creates loopholes for denying customary law on the grounds that it is "not in keeping with current developments."

Ironically, the definitions of "living" and "thriving" are often monopolized by bureaucracies unfamiliar with the social realities of indigenous communities. Consequently, communities that still practice customary law are often deemed administratively ineligible simply because they lack formal documentation or a modern organizational structure. This is where the state forces customary law to resemble state institutions, rather than respecting its unique nature.

In fact, from agrarian conflicts to inheritance disputes, from customary land agreements to social sanction systems, customary law has proven effective in maintaining local order and justice. Various studies have shown that customary-based resolutions tend to be faster, less expensive, and oriented toward restoring social relations, rather than simply punishing.

For example, in many indigenous communities in Kalimantan and Sumatra, violations of customary law are resolved through open deliberation and symbolic restoration, prioritizing harmony. Contrast this with the national court system, which often positions disputing parties as adversaries. Here, customary law appears to operate not on the basis of victory, but on the restoration and strengthening of social bonds.

In the modern context, we can no longer rely on state law as the sole arbiter of justice. We need an inclusive legal system that doesn't position tradition as a dead archaeology, but as a source of ethical inspiration and contemporary legal practice. Customary law should not be merely remembered as academic romanticism but must be an active part of the national legal policy-making process.

In closing this chapter, I would like to emphasize: customary law is not merely an addition to the national legal mosaic, but rather a historical foundation that needs to be revived with just policies and an open perspective. In customary law, we find not only traces of the past but also the possibility of a more humane and contextual legal future.

However, challenges to the existence of customary law come not only from the state, but also from internal changes within indigenous communities themselves. Modernization, migration, and market intervention have eroded many old structures. Younger generations in many communities no longer fully understand the customary legal institutions inherited from their ancestors. In some cases, customary law is seen as a burden, something that hinders "progress" because it is deemed inconsistent with market logic and the national legal system.

This situation is exacerbated by the lack of documentation and participatory codification of customary law. When the state attempts to incorporate customary law into its formal legal framework, it often simplifies or even distorts its core values. As a result, what is referred to as "customary law" in official documents sometimes no longer reflects the authentic practices that live within the community.

As a lawyer who has been directly involved in advocating for the rights of indigenous peoples, I have witnessed this dilemma firsthand. On the one hand, customary law has strong moral force and social legitimacy. But on the other hand, when confronted with state law, it is like a guest invited but never truly welcomed. Courts often dismiss customary-based arguments simply because they are not framed within a positivist framework.

In fact, if we honestly look back at the history of Indonesian law before colonialism, it was customary law that governed people's lives fairly and wisely. Colonialism, which brought a foreign legal system, gradually removed customary law from the center of legal decision-making. After independence, we inherited that system, unconsciously perpetuating the subordination of our own ancestral laws.

We need to rethink. Is it possible to build a truly Indonesian national legal system without placing customary law as its pillar? Is justice only attainable through the toga, the judge's gavel, and the statute book, or rather through deliberation, the words of elders, and the customs that live within the people's daily lives?

In my many travels across the archipelago—from the mountains of Toraja to the jungles of the interior of Kalimantan—I have found a common thread: people's trust in the law is measured not by the formulation of articles, but by a living sense of justice. They don't demand grandiose courts or lengthy procedures, but rather justice experienced and implemented by those who understand the local context and communal values. That is the power of customary law, which formal legal systems often lack.

Unfortunately, the national legal framework has not yet given equal recognition to this system. Even when the Constitutional Court or laws recognize the existence of indigenous communities, implementation at the regional and bureaucratic levels is often fraught with obstacles. Administrative recognition becomes a barrier that blocks customary rights simply because formal documentation is lacking—yet the essence of customary law lies not in documents, but in collective practice and understanding.

The neglect of customary law is not only a matter of injustice, but also a loss of Indonesia's legal identity. A great nation is not merely one capable of imitating foreign systems, but one capable of nurturing local wisdom as its foundation. When customary law is sidelined, we are essentially tearing apart the roots of our own legal history.

As lawyers, I believe our duty is not only to defend clients in court, but also to fight to ensure our legal system retains its soul. Indigenous peoples are not merely objects of legal aid, but sources of legal knowledge themselves. They are the rightful owners of Indonesia's justice narrative.

Behind the rampant violations of customary territories and the disregard for the rights of traditional communities lies an irony that cannot be ignored: the state is quicker to grant concession permits to corporations than to acknowledge the existence of indigenous communities who have lived on these lands for centuries. In some cases, positive law has even become a tool of legitimacy to displace customary law. Herein lies the absurdity of our law: it speaks of justice in formal legal language, but fails to capture the sense of justice that lives within the people.

I once witnessed a trial where indigenous people wept because their ancestral land, which had been passed down through generations, was deemed "legally void" due to the lack of a certificate. The judge who ruled on the case may not have intended to harm, but the system that gave rise to it has long been blind to local realities. We are trapped in a colonial legal logic that requires everything to be proven with documents, even though the truth of life is not always contained in paper files.

Therefore, the struggle to revive customary law is not merely about protecting minorities, but about repairing the foundations of a national legal system that has been limping for too long. In indigenous communities, law not only regulates but also nurtures. It is not a tool of power, but rather a means of maintaining balance between humans, nature, and ancestral spirits. This balance has long been missing from our often rigid and transactional legal system.

If we want national law to truly side with justice, we must begin by listening to the deepest voices of our own cultural roots. Customary law is not an outdated relic to be kept in a museum. It is a living legacy, waiting to be recognized, embraced, and empowered as part of Indonesia's comprehensive legal architecture.

In my numerous encounters with traditional leaders, I've noticed that they aren't demanding that the state submit to customary law, but rather that the state be an equal and respectful partner. They aren't anti-modernity, nor do they reject national law. What they seek is recognition of their existence as legitimate and dignified legal subjects.

Ironically, while the international community is beginning to look at local wisdom systems as an alternative to restorative justice, we are reluctant to look inward. Developed nations are beginning to learn from the principles of deliberation, reconciliation, and balance between nature that have been part of our customary law for centuries. Meanwhile, we, the direct inheritors of those traditions, still doubt their value, or even deride them as "unmodern."

We cannot deny that the customary legal system has been shaken, fragmented by colonialism and post-independence distortions. However, this does not mean it is dead. What is needed today is political and intellectual courage to revitalize customary law, not by standardizing it in a cold document, but by bringing it closer to the real lives of the people who practice it.

If this nation truly desires to build a legal system with a distinct cultural identity, then customary law is a foundation that must not be neglected. This is not only to honor our ancestors, but also to design a just, humane, and contextual legal future. And this must begin now, before the remaining legacy is completely buried by time and our own indifference.

In many parts of the Indonesian archipelago, customary law still lives on—not just as a collective memory, but as a way of life. It shapes village governance, regulates land affairs, and even resolves family and social conflicts in a more peaceful and deeply rooted manner. Unfortunately, however, this system often operates "on the fringes of the state"—as if merely an accessory, not part of a legitimate justice system.

In fact, in some respects, customary law mechanisms are more progressive than formal law. For example, in terms of victim reparation, community involvement, or principles of balance that go beyond punishment to restoring social relations. Customary law doesn't just look at who is at fault, but also how the wrong can be resolved for the common good.

However, the sustainability of customary law faces significant pressure from the centralization of state law, bureaucratic egos, and a uniform development mindset. When a conflict arises in a traditional village, state officials prefer to ignore the role of traditional elders and directly apply the Criminal Code, without dialogue and context. This not only uproots the community's social roots but also negates local potential to foster justice.

It's time for the state to stop treating customary law as a mere cultural ornament. It's not a folkloric display to attract tourists, nor is it a commodity for arts festivals. Customary law is a living and relevant social structure. It can serve as a bridge between society and the state, between formal justice and substantive justice.

However, the state's failure to integrate customary law is not simply a matter of ignorance or administrative negligence. It reflects a perspective that often measures the value of a system based on Western modernity. When modernization is the sole standard, anything born from local wisdom is deemed outdated, even though it may be more in tune with the needs of the community.

Customary justice does not require lawyers in the formal sense, but rather mediation based on friendship. It does not recognize punitive fines, but rather compensation tailored to the social context. In some cases, customary law has even provided long-term solutions to agrarian conflicts, inheritance disputes, and inter-community disputes—without the high cost and layered bureaucracy.

Unfortunately, many traditional leaders no longer receive the respect they deserve. They are considered symbols, not driving forces.

Yet, they are the last line of defense when state law fails to reach or engage communities at the grassroots level. While formal courts are preoccupied with piles of files and political agendas, traditional elders quietly resolve cases with their conscience.

Even as a lawyer, I've learned many clearer legal lessons from conversations with traditional leaders than from international law seminars. They don't speak Latin, don't cite foreign jurisprudence, but they truly understand what justice is. For them, law isn't about rules, but about maintaining balance in life.

## CHAPTER 8

### A Viral Case, Justice That Came Too Late

In the age of social media, justice often takes place behind the camera. It comes after netizens' voices echo, after hashtags trend, and after public emotions run high. Ironically, it's not legal mechanisms that first respond to victims' cries, but algorithms.

Cases that have lain untouched for years can suddenly reach the courtroom simply because of a two-minute video. From street assaults to harassment in educational institutions, the same pattern repeats itself: justice prevails when the cameras are on, not when the law is supposed to operate. This is not evidence of the success of digital democracy, but rather a sign that our legal system is slow, even negligent, until forced to succumb to public pressure.

I once handled a case where the victim had filed multiple police reports. There was no meaningful response. But when footage of the incident went viral, there was action. The police arrived, the media arrived, and officials began to speak. It all felt like a charade fueled by shame—not a sense of justice.

Virality has replaced procedure. We live in an age where "legal responses" have become a form of response, not moral reflection. Many victims finally get justice, not because the system works, but because the public cries out loud enough to be ignored. And when that happens, the public wonders: is this justice, or just a panicked response to the spotlight?

Many also question the integrity of law enforcement officers' intentions when a new case gains attention after going viral. This phenomenon creates a new dilemma: the perception that the value of a person's life is determined by the explosive power of their content. Justice must take precedence over trends.

In many cases, those with access to media and digital networks are more likely to be heard. But what about those without mobile phones, unable to create long threads, or lacking the skills to reach the hearts of netizens? Justice becomes selective, not because the law requires it, but because the digital platform only gives space to those who have been highlighted.

I've also witnessed how some criminals suddenly become "framing victims" simply because they were able to change public perception. Herein lies the paradox: when perception is more decisive than evidence, and mass emotion is stronger than legal logic.

The biggest challenge we face is not just improving the legal system, but also restoring trust that justice doesn't have to go viral. That the state must act swiftly, not out of shame, but out of concern. That every victim's voice—even if unheard on social media—must still have weight in the courtroom.

In the rush to respond to public opinion, the legal process sometimes loses its balance. Some cases are expedited due to pressure, while others are dismissed due to lack of viral appeal. Herein lies a deeper problem: justice is forced to become selective, dependent on the spotlight, on trends.

We've witnessed previously passive law enforcement suddenly become active when a case attracts national or international attention. However, the public demands not just swift action, but also consistency. Justice is not only for those capable of causing online commotion, but also for those who can only cry in silence.

This phenomenon also demonstrates the immense power of the digital community in influencing the direction of law enforcement. But this power is paradoxical: it can be a beacon of light that exposes injustice, but it can also be a fire that burns reputations without complete facts. This is where the law is tested—not just in its text, but in its steadfastness in standing amidst a storm of opinion.

As a lawyer, I believe the law should not bend to trends, but it should also not be deaf to the cries of the people. It must be upright, but also responsive. It must be fair, but also humane. Therefore, when we talk about justice arriving late, we are actually acknowledging that there is something more painful than injustice: justice displayed solely for the sake of image.

In several cases I've handled and observed, clients often only receive proper legal treatment after their cases become public. Before that, they're just numbers in reports, or worse, ignored because they're deemed to have no social leverage. We've reached a point where social media feeds can be more effective than formal appeals.

Of course, not every case can, or even should, go viral. But today's reality means many people are "fighting to be heard" not through formal legal mechanisms, but through publicity strategies, campaigns, and mass sympathy. The law has become a stage—not an arena for objective consideration, but rather a subjective spectacle driven by popularity, not priorities.

I'm not blaming the public for speaking out or the journalists for reporting. In fact, they often serve as the first bridge for those unable to access legal assistance. But our system must be more robust than simply responding to viral pressure. It must be a living system, present even when there are no cameras or trending hashtags.

This is a call for the state, the judiciary, and all legal practitioners to reflect: Do we operate only when the spotlight is on? Should justice await signals from algorithms? Or are we capable of shining the light of law from within, even when cyberspace is silent?

In various legal discussion forums I attend, I often hear the complaint from both senior practitioners and young activists: "Why do we have to wait for public outrage for the system to work?" This question evokes a collective unease. It's not just a critique of institutions, but also a profound reflection on how we, as a nation, value the importance of justice.

One case after another reveals a painful pattern. Only when a victim of sexual violence speaks out on social media does a serious investigation begin. Only when a video of the abuse goes viral does the authorities act swiftly. It's as if, until it goes viral, justice can be delayed or negotiated.

There's a sharp irony here. Once, people trusted the judiciary as their last resort. Now, many rely on cell phone cameras and the luck of algorithms. As a lawyer, I feel called not only to accompany clients in the courtroom, but also to bear witness to a time when justice requires likes to move forward.

But amidst all this, I still believe. I believe that from the growing public unrest and legal awareness, a push for systemic change will emerge. I believe that behind the media hype, there remains a genuine desire for improvement. And I believe that all of us, in our respective roles, can ensure that the law is not only present when things go viral, but also present whenever it's needed.

In my observations as a lawyer and writer who frequently works directly with the public, I see how distrust in legal institutions is not just a sentiment, but a recurring experience. People who have reported, waited, and ultimately given up—because their cases haven't been processed—slowly form a collective trauma. When the legal process is slow, when perpetrators are in power and victims have no voice, social media becomes a cheap but effective last resort.

One thing worth highlighting is that justice in our system remains responsive, not preventative. This means that law enforcement is only implemented when there is significant pressure. In fact, the value of justice should be inherent in every legal action, not sought only when there is already chaos.

This phenomenon also reveals how social media has transformed into an alternative courtroom where people can try, defend, or condemn individuals in a matter of minutes. On the one hand, this reflects the dynamics of open digital democracy. On the other hand, there is a significant risk that viral pressure will override principles of justice, such as the presumption of innocence and legal protection for all parties.

As a lawyer, I strive to balance the two. I believe that digital power can be a tool for legal education, not just a tool for pressure. I frequently present legal cases in content, so that the public not only feels anger but also understanding. My hope is that from every viral outcry, a deeper understanding will grow.

What's needed now is not just a responsive legal system, but one that has the courage to listen before all eyes are on it. We need judges and prosecutors who are sensitive to small voices, not just when they've already become loud. We need police who act swiftly, not because of trending topics, but because of morality and professionalism. And more importantly, we need the courage to make amends before it's too late.

We have entered an era where the voice of the people can be heard louder on Twitter than in a courtroom. When people feel that formal institutions are not responding quickly enough to injustice, they turn to social media—tweeting, posting, tagging public accounts, and creating hashtags that generate storms of opinion. Ironically, it is precisely in the delays in formal legal proceedings that social media raises hopes for justice, though often in an inaccurate form.

However, from a lawyer's perspective, I can see two sides to this phenomenon. Social media can indeed be a tool for advocacy, even public protection, but it can also be a double-edged sword. When netizens judge before the courts have ruled, when public sympathy determines the direction of the investigation, the law is no longer based on evidence, but on emotion. This is dangerous. We don't want to replace slow justice with a wild trial.

However, I don't deny that some victims actually got their rights because of going viral. I once handled a case that was nearly frozen—witnesses were silenced, the complainant was intimidated, and evidence was "lost." However, after being reported and brought to the digital space, the case was reinstated. Public scrutiny forced the system to move. This is the reality: in many situations, justice requires a spotlight.

But the question is: does it have to go viral to get justice? Should victims make crying videos first? Does it have to be trending to demand safety and dignity?

If the answer is yes, then something is fundamentally wrong with our system. The law should protect everyone, not just those who can stir up trouble online. And our collective responsibility—as citizens, legal practitioners, policymakers, and even social media users—is to build a culture of justice that doesn't require virality to move the needle. Because justice that arrives late, even when it finally arrives, still leaves scars.

Many parties also exploit "virality" as a strategy. Legal aid organizations, activists, and even attorneys are sometimes forced to manipulate public opinion to gain the attention of authorities. I've personally been approached by victims' families begging for "help to make their cases go viral" because they've exhausted conventional methods—reporting to the police, sending letters to state institutions, and even going to the local parliament. They said, "Sir, if we don't go viral, we're afraid our children will be forgotten."

These statements struck a chord in me. Not because they blame the law, but because they demonstrate the vast distance between the people and the system that is supposed to protect them.

Does this mean the law has been paralyzed? No. But it is faltering. It's plodding along in a fast-paced world. In an age where news can spread in five seconds, our law still has to wait for administrative processes that can take weeks. This is where the trust gap grows.

And when trust is lost, people seek other avenues. They seek justice through the pressure of opinion, not through the courts.

As a lawyer who also lives in the digital world, I believe that social media can be both an ally and a reminder to the legal system. But it should not replace legal logic. Not everything that goes viral is true.

Not everything that remains silent is wrong. That's why the law must be reformed—so that justice doesn't depend on algorithms, but on the principle of truth.

The public's increasing reliance on "trial by internet" is inextricably linked to limited access to fair and prompt legal aid. For many, especially those living far from large cities, the only way to pressure law enforcement is to make their case public. In an ideal legal system, facts and evidence should be sufficient to uphold justice. However, in practice, public pressure often becomes additional evidence.

We've seen many cases only receive serious action after going viral—whether it's due to a viral video, a lengthy social media thread, or an online petition garnering thousands of signatures. This phenomenon seems to create parallel trials: one in the courtroom and one on your timeline. While not necessarily a bad thing, it opens the door to manipulation, provocation, and the judgment of opinion unfounded by legal facts.

Admittedly, public pressure through virality can sometimes be a lifeline for those marginalized. It acts as a megaphone for voices that have previously gone unheard. It gives a platform to stories that would otherwise be buried by bureaucracy and power. But the question is: do we want our justice system to depend on how "compelling" a case is to the public?

This is the major challenge for the future of our legal system—building a strong, transparent, and responsive system so that people don't have to rely on virality as a prerequisite for justice. Justice should be neutral to the spotlight and not biased toward popularity. It must stand tall, even when no one is watching.

# CHAPTER 9
## Tradition, Trauma, and Legal Transformation

Behind every legal system lies a long history filled with wounds, hopes, and struggles. Indonesia is no exception. The laws we inherit today are not only the result of rational and technocratic processes, but also the product of a clash of ideas, traditions, and past traumas that have yet to fully heal. From oppressive colonial laws to faltering reforms, each stage has left its mark on our legal structure—both in the form of rules and in how we interpret justice.

Local legal traditions, such as customary law and cultural values, are often positioned as mere complements—not foundations. Yet, in Javanese, Bugis, Batak, Dayak, Balinese, and even Papuan societies, conflict resolution systems have been passed down through generations, each with its own distinct social logic. These systems may not be documented in official state documents, but they live on in the memories and everyday actions of society. When state law fails, they become the ultimate anchor.

However, our history has left us with trauma. The oppression of the people by colonial law, the use of law as a tool of power during the New Order, and the slow process of legal reform in the democratic era have caused public distrust. Many people feel the law is not on their side. This is not simply a procedural issue—it is a profound psychological and cultural one.

Legal transformation, if it is to be truly realized, must involve a process of collective healing. Laws cannot be revised merely in the boardroom; they must be restored in the hearts of the people. We need a reconciliation between state law and societal law. This involves not only revising articles one by one, but also rebuilding the relationship between the state and its citizens based on a sense of justice.

True transformation means creating laws that are not only formally valid but also socially valid. This means that laws must be presented with a human face—not merely as texts, but as just experiences. We cannot build the future of law without acknowledging the wounds of the past, respecting traditions, and being willing to change.

Most legal failures in Indonesia are not simply due to a lack of regulation, but to a lack of resonance between the law and the collective consciousness of society. When law is seen as something "external"—a product of the state, officials, or elites—it becomes alien. People feel they have no stake, no ownership, and ultimately no trust.

Yet, in Javanese culture, law is more than just prohibitions and sanctions. Law is embedded in values such as tepa slira (tolerance), rukun (harmony), and paseduluran (brotherhood). These values form a social structure that respects peace, not through coercion, but through awareness. This is what I call living law—a law that grows from below, not from above.

However, historical trauma has made this law, which was originally organic and derived from local values, rigid and alienating. When the colonial legal system entered and replaced customary law, the logic of "control" replaced the logic of "protection." Law became a tool for regulation, not for care. And post-independence legal transformation has not fully succeeded in reversing this paradigm.

For this reason, future legal transformation must encompass three axes: recognition, healing, and unification.

- **Confession**means recognizing local legal heritages as a legitimate part of the national legal system.
- **Healing**means addressing the collective wounds of past injustices, both through historical honesty and inclusive healing mechanisms.
- **Unification**means re-stitching the relationship between society and law, making law not only a symbol of the state, but also a reflection of the nation's conscience.

Indonesia's legal transformation will not succeed if it is led solely by technocrats. It must be driven by feelings: shame when the law is abused, anger when justice is betrayed, and a deep love for this nation.

Legal transformation isn't just about changing articles or reforming the justice system. It's about rebuilding trust that has been shattered. Law doesn't live only in courtrooms—it lives in markets, homes, villages, and the minds of ordinary people. So when people are still afraid to go to the police station, or when a report isn't considered important until it goes viral, it's not just a procedural crisis, but an existential one: the law is no longer trusted as a guardian of justice, but as a tool of power.

This is where collective trauma comes into play. Many indigenous peoples and ordinary citizens inherit intergenerational memories of injustice: land seized without compensation, perpetrators of crimes who go unpunished because of their close ties to the elite, or victims of abuse forced into silence because the system protects the perpetrators. All of this creates an emotional distance between the people and the law.

Local legal traditions that once thrived on the spirit of mutual cooperation and deliberation are slowly being replaced by laws that feel impersonal and technocratic. On the one hand, modernization brings certainty and systematicity. But on the other, it erodes the distinctive values of the archipelago that give justice a human face. In the future transformation, what is needed is not the elimination of traditional heritage, but rather wise integration. We must no longer be trapped in the dichotomy between "custom" and "state," between "traditional" and "modern." In fact, Indonesian law will be stronger if it can harmonize the two.

My experience as a lawyer working directly in various regions shows that national law is only effective if it taps into the cultural pulse of the community. In an inheritance case in an East Javanese village, for example, the settlement was actually carried out according to customary law, and all parties agreed. However, because it wasn't legally recognized, the case dragged on in court for years. Isn't this ironic?

We need a legal system that is more culturally flexible yet remains firm in principle. The law must be able to protect without ignoring modern structures. This is where healing our legal trauma as a nation becomes crucial: acknowledging past mistakes, restoring trust, and creating real participation for indigenous peoples, women, marginalized groups, and the younger generation in shaping the future of law.

However, transformation will not happen simply by changing laws. It requires a shift in mindset—both from those in positions of power and from communities that have been marginalized. We need a generation of legal leaders who understand not only the text but also the context; who don't just memorize articles but also understand feelings.

Legal trauma passed down from generation to generation can only be healed through openness and the courage to listen to voices that have been silenced. When victims of human rights violations, indigenous peoples, and minority groups are given space to speak out and are respected as equal legal subjects, the healing process begins.

This is where the importance of legal education that is inseparable from cultural roots lies. Law students should not only be taught to prepare lawsuits or defense memos, but also learn to listen to the public's complaints, understand the symbolic language of tradition, and sense the pulse of justice from corners untouched by media cameras.

The transformation of Indonesian law will only succeed if we dare to be humble: to accept that our system has (and still is) harmful, that law is not always present in the form of the state, and that justice does not have to wait for the hammer to strike. True justice grows when we are able to humanize the law—transforming it from oppressive power into an embracing hope.

# CHAPTER 10

## The Javanese Culture of Silence and Submission

If there's one profound characteristic that manifests in every Javanese breath, it's silence. Silence isn't just about not speaking, but a form of communication deeply fraught with meaning. In Javanese culture, silence often speaks louder than speech. It holds contemplation, caution, and sometimes, unspoken wounds.

Giving in doesn't mean losing. In Javanese philosophy, giving in is a form of wisdom. Javanese people believe that controlling anger is a form of strength. A person who can restrain themselves—not explode, not react emotionally—is someone who has triumphed over themselves. In everyday language, we know the expression, alon-alon waton kelakon—slowly but surely. However, in the legal world, this culture can be a dangerous paradox.

When victims of violence choose to remain silent for fear of embarrassing their families; when indigenous communities remain silent when their land is seized; when women who are victims of abuse choose to accept the situation out of shame—that is where silence becomes a trap. It becomes a barrier to justice.

The culture of giving in, which initially served as a form of politeness and respect, has become a collective psychological burden passed down through generations. In courtrooms, this culture of silence translates into a withdrawal from the legal process. In politics, it becomes a lack of courage to speak up for one's rights. In the home, it becomes a chasm separating pain from self-defense.

As a lawyer born into Javanese culture, I don't see this as a disgrace. In fact, this is where the beauty lies: understanding that behind silence lies extraordinary inner depth. However, this culture should not be used as a shield to silence. It must be transformed—into conscious silence, not passive; into strategic yielding, not surrendering.

Javanese people are taught to maintain harmony. But a false harmony, built on silenced suffering, is not true peace. True peace is possible only with justice. And justice is born only from the courage to speak out—even if trembling, even if alone.

But silence maintained for too long can become a legacy of trauma. We see generation after generation growing up with similar patterns: harboring hurt, delaying anger, suppressing feelings of injustice, to avoid conflict. Even in law enforcement, many come with quiet expressions: "I don't want to escalate the problem," or "I can't bear to go against my own family." These statements are not signs of legal maturity, but rather a reflection of cultural pressure to always be protective, to protect the feelings of everyone but themselves.

Why is this important in a legal context? Because the legal system cannot operate on shame. It requires the courage to reveal the truth, even when it hurts. A culture of silence has left many violations hidden, unaddressed, and ultimately become inherited social wounds. This is the critical point: when culture is no longer a protector of values, but an obstacle to justice.

As a lawyer who understands local values, I believe that approaching Javanese society cannot rely solely on articles. We need to analyze the issues with empathy, in a way that doesn't threaten harmony but still encourages courage to speak up. Educate people that revealing the truth doesn't mean being disrespectful. Voicing one's rights isn't a form of defiance. Rather, it's part of upholding dignity and a sense of justice.

Silence may be a way to calm a storm, but not to build a future. Giving in may be a form of love, but it shouldn't be a way to allow injustice to prevail. And our task as the next generation of legal advocates is to bridge these local values with universal principles of justice—so that the harmony we strive for is not merely silence, but a serenity born of courage and truth.

In the process of character formation in Javanese law, we're not just talking about norms and rules, but also about feelings of shame, fear of disappointing parents, or even resentment toward neighbors.

When conflict arises, the consideration is often not "who's right" but "what will people think?" The law becomes mired in fear of ridicule, not justice.

In court, I often witness clients abandoning their rights simply because the opposing party is a relative, neighbor, or old acquaintance. "I'm afraid it will disturb my extended family," or "let me give in, as long as it's peaceful." These phrases seem to become a collective mantra. However, in the long run, this pattern actually creates inequality: those who dare to violate will continue to prosper, while those who remain silent continue to bear the burden.

This culture does indeed create a society full of courtesy and tolerance. However, when it's used as a shield to cover wounds or avoid accountability, it becomes a system of silencing. We cannot deny our roots, but we can choose how to proceed. Silence is no longer golden when it becomes a tool of oppression. Giving in is no longer noble when it buryes justice.

So our task going forward is not to erase local culture, but to reimagine it. We need legal education that embraces the values of tepa selira while still upholding transparency. We need legal reform that understands that in the Javanese context, an emotional approach is often more effective than a purely normative one. And we need collective courage to speak out: that telling the truth does not mean disobedience, that demanding justice does not mean going against tradition.

With this awareness, hopefully, future generations will no longer see silence and giving in as the only options. Instead, they will know when it's time to take a stand, speak up, and stand up for themselves, others, and a more just future.

However, it's important to emphasize: silence and giving in are not weaknesses. In certain contexts, this attitude reflects social maturity and extraordinary fortitude. Javanese people have long understood that not all battles must be won with loud voices—there are times when silence is the way to dampen the fire, and giving in is the highest form of inner strength.

However, in an increasingly complex and digitally connected world, where injustice can easily spread in a matter of seconds, silence can be fatal. Individuals who remain silent for too long can miss opportunities to save themselves—and societies that give in for too long can lose their way to justice.

This pattern is also evident in legal proceedings at the village level, where traditional leaders or elders are often given more respect than formal legal instruments. Conflict resolution processes are carried out using a family-friendly approach, but often result in the victim's rights being ignored. Especially when the perpetrator is a prominent figure or close relative, silence is not the result of spiritual reflection, but rather a product of social pressure.

If left unchecked, this culture of silence could become a chain holding back the pace of legal change toward substantive justice. The public needs to be encouraged to speak out, to express their hurt, and to demand their rights without feeling guilty. This is not just the task of lawyers, activists, or academics, but also ours as part of the culture itself.

The silence and submissiveness deeply rooted in Javanese culture have an ambiguous role in shaping the legal character of society. On the one hand, it creates a society that is patient, restrained, and avoids open conflict. However, on the other hand, this attitude can also give rise to systemic inequality—because powerlessness tends to be silenced by the habit of "nrimo ing pandum," accepting fate as inevitable.

In many of the cases I handle, especially in villages or small communities, I often encounter victims who don't report the incident because they don't want to embarrass their families or because they feel they don't deserve to seek justice. They choose to remain silent—not because they don't know they've been wronged, but because they believe that exposing the problem will only worsen their social situation.

Furthermore, giving in also becomes a survival mechanism amidst power imbalances. When someone knows the perpetrator has an insider or comes from a prominent family, they feel that resisting is futile. The safest option, then, is to remain silent and pray that the universe will take care of them.

However, from a just and progressive legal perspective, the courage to speak up is the first step in restructuring justice itself. The law cannot work if society is shaped to distrust it. Therefore, our task—as lawyers, educators, writers, and fellow citizens—is to create a safe space for voices that have been held back.

Interestingly, this culture of silence doesn't just exist at the grassroots level. Even within bureaucracies and law enforcement agencies themselves, a culture of silence exists regarding unethical practices—either due to fear of consequences or due to being trapped in a system of mutual protection. Thus, silence becomes systemic. Compromise becomes the norm.

Ultimately, silence and yielding are not simply personal choices in Javanese culture—they are a collective legacy rooted in social relations, power, and how we understand conflict. But in a world that is constantly evolving and demands openness, these values cannot be left to stand alone without context. If not paired with the courage to speak up and defend what is right, silence will only become a silence that delays justice. Therefore, the task of today's generation is not to eliminate ancestral culture, but to reinterpret it in the light of the times: that silence may be wise, but speaking is a sign of a living conscience.

# CHAPTER 11

## Becoming a Lawyer in a Cultured Country

Becoming a lawyer in Indonesia isn't just about memorizing laws, winning cases, or crafting legal arguments before a panel of judges. In a country as culturally rich as Indonesia, a lawyer's role is more complex—they must understand not only written law but also local values, cultural symbols, and the moral language of the community. This is a field not found in law school but rather emerges in real-life interactions with clients, indigenous communities, authorities, and fellow justice seekers.

Indonesia is not a country devoid of social heritage. Here, the word "polite" can be more important than "correct"; and sometimes "peace" is prioritized over "court decisions." In such a realm, a lawyer cannot simply think in legalistic terms. They are required to be cultural spokespersons, interpreters of social meaning, and sometimes—ironically—mediators between legal texts and the reality of life, which is not always law-abiding.

I myself have often faced the dilemma of whether to follow legal procedures precisely or listen to the inner voice of clients who desire justice more than mere compensation. Clients from Javanese backgrounds, for example, often come not immediately seeking victory, but rather ensuring that their cause remains within the realm of eling lan waspada (mindfulness and vigilance)—aware of their position and wise in their actions.

Being a lawyer in a cultured country is the art of remaining firm without losing empathy, upholding the law without abandoning local wisdom, and standing before clients as both a legal advocate and a guardian of their social dignity. In many cases, a cultural approach actually opens the way to more meaningful resolutions than lengthy, cold litigation filled with formalities.

In this country, law is not just about what's written in the state gazette, but also about what lives in the hearts of its people. And here, an Indonesian lawyer must find their way between articles and feelings, between the system and conscience.

Amidst all the developments and digitalization of law, we still live in a country that respects etiquette, upholds good manners, and values the balance between rights and obligations, not merely because of rules, but because of compassion. Therefore, being a lawyer in such a country is not just about conveying legal facts, but how to convey them while maintaining the face of the opponent, the dignity of the client, and respect for the court and the public.

I often encounter cases that are legally very strong to win, but culturally and socially can be damaging to relationships between families, neighbors, and even indigenous communities. This is where a lawyer's non-legal skills are put to the test. The ability to read the situation, understand local values, and bridge the gap between legal and cultural logic determines the direction of the struggle.

A lawyer in Indonesia, especially one who frequently works with grassroots communities or indigenous communities, must be able to interpret values. For example, in inheritance cases, customary land disputes, or customary violations, we cannot simply measure everything by court decisions. We must listen to the unspoken voices—the voices of our ancestors, the voices of our ancestors, and the voices passed down through songs, wisdom, or even silent glances.

This doesn't mean we ignore state law, but rather enrich legal practice so it doesn't become stifled, so it remains alive and accepted by society. Culturally savvy lawyers can explain each article with down-to-earth analogies: equating the concept of due process with the customary village consultation, equating the principle of presumption of innocence with the philosophy of "aja mung nyawang sakarep dhewe."

Moreover, in a pluralistic country like Indonesia, lawyers often serve as bridges between state law and customary law, between universal and local values. Sensitivity to cultural context is not a weakness, but rather a key weapon in the fight for justice that is not only legal but also legitimate in the eyes of society.

My experience as a lawyer working directly in various regions of Indonesia has taught me one important lesson: justice isn't just about winning or losing, but about maintaining harmony. In small villages, in remote areas untouched by the news, legal decisions can be more meaningful when they prevent the breakdown of family relationships than simply winning a lawsuit.

I once handled a land dispute between two brothers on the south coast of Java. Legally, my client had all the necessary documentation and could easily have won in court. However, during the mediation process, I chose a more hands-on approach: approaching village elders, listening to oral traditions, and respecting deeply rooted cultural traditions. The result? The case was resolved amicably, without the need for a judge's gavel. The two families were able to sit together at the next religious holiday.

In a cultured nation, victory achieved without leaving social scars is a true victory. This is what I call a "cultural victory"—a victory that unites, not divides.

For me, being a lawyer in Indonesia is about re-weaving social fabrics that may have been torn by conflict, not simply winning cases. Lawyers are not only legal experts, but also guardians of values. We are not just defenders of the law, but also guardians of tradition, transmitters of wisdom, and bridges between modernity and ancestral heritage.

Being a lawyer in a cultured country is more than just a profession—it's a calling to bridge the gap between written law and the law lived within society. In Indonesia, where national law meets custom, and modern logic coexists with spiritual values, lawyers are required to possess cultural sensitivity, social wisdom, and moral courage.

Legal science must be flexible—not to compromise on principle, but to address the realities of a diverse society. In practice, lawyers are required not only to understand the articles but also to master communication, community psychology, and social ethnography. They must understand that behind every dispute lies a larger narrative than mere legality.

In this context, a lawyer cannot simply be equipped with jurisprudence and legal doctrine. He must learn to listen like a puppeteer listens to a gamelan orchestra—with sensitivity, patience, and a trained intuition. He must be able to discern when to speak out and when to remain silent for the common good.

A lawyer who truly understands his nation's culture will not be easily seduced by the glitz of mere formal victory. He will see beyond that—that in every legal decision lies an opportunity to restore dignity, rebuild relationships, and set an example that law doesn't always have to take the form of a verdict. It can take the form of reconciliation, recognition, and justice that favors wisdom.

So, being a lawyer in a cultured country is an honor, as well as a big responsibility. Not only because we guard the law, but because we guard the true meaning of justice: justice that cares for, not destroys.

# CHAPTER 12

## Learning Law Rooted in the Spirit of the Javanese Nation and Culture

Learning law isn't simply about copying articles from textbooks into your brain, but rather about internalizing the values that inform the society in which the law is implemented. In this country, especially in Java, law doesn't grow in a vacuum, but rather from cultural roots that predate the state and formal legal institutions. The spirit of this nation—rooted in the values of mutual cooperation, etiquette, and the philosophy of manunggaling kawula lan gusti—gives its own color to how we interpret justice.

For Javanese people, law is not a rigid instrument of coercion. It is a way of life, part of social harmony, where conflicts are sought to be reconciled, not won. This is where the importance of studying law lies in its cultural context. For without cultural roots, law loses its soul—it becomes harsh, cold, and alien to its own society.

Therefore, this chapter invites us to delve into how to study law holistically: not only with logic and reason, but also with feeling, empathy, and sensitivity to the soul of the nation. How can legal knowledge be combined with local wisdom? How can Javanese values such as rukun (harmony), tepa salira (compassion), and laku simpati (compassionate behavior) inspire a more humane legal practice? And how can a new generation of legal scholars reclaim law from the soil they stand on—rather than simply importing a system that ignores their cultural roots?

In the context of Javanese culture, law is practice, not merely articles. It lives in speech and actions. When someone speaks gently, without immediately passing judgment, but instead invites a heart-to-heart conversation, they are truly enforcing law rooted in feeling, not just reason. Law, from a Javanese perspective, is about protecting, not merely punishing. It embodies the hope of restoring relationships, not merely the punishment that cuts them off.

In Javanese villages, the practice of customary deliberation remains alive, though it is slowly eroding. Institutions such as village councils (rembugan desa), community forums (rukun warga), and community leaders such as the village head (modin), traditional leaders, and village elders often act as mediators in resolving disputes before they reach the formal legal realm. This system is not only efficient but also touches on the emotional roots and relationships between residents.

Unfortunately, modern legal education systems often break this bond. Law students are taught foreign jurisprudence, Western theory, and national legal systems based on legal positivism. This is not wrong, as formal legal systems do rely on structure and procedures. However, what is often absent is a space to understand law as culture—as something that grows out of society itself.

A prospective lawyer, prosecutor, judge, or legal academic who doesn't understand their own culture risks being the fire extinguisher who ends up pouring gasoline on the fire. When they apply the law rigidly without considering local values and social emotions, they lose public trust. This is where it's crucial to contextualize legal knowledge within the lived realities of society—returning law to its cultural roots.

In Javanese culture, the philosophy of sangkan paraning dumadi (the origin and purpose of humankind) teaches that all actions must be grounded in spiritual and social awareness. Even those seeking justice must reflect on their intentions: is it out of revenge, or a desire to create peace? These values, if internalized by law enforcement, will result in policies that are not only legal but also dignified.

Amidst the rapid flow of globalization, legal education cannot simply be modeled on the West, let alone abandon local values. Living law is law that grows from the land we walk on and the heavens we uphold. Therefore, studying law for Indonesians, especially those rooted in Javanese culture, should not be merely about memorizing articles and jurisprudence, but also about absorbing local wisdom, understanding the meaning of symbols, and developing sensitivity to conflicts stemming from complex social relations.

The attitude of eling lan waspada—awareness and vigilance—in Javanese philosophy should be a fundamental principle for every law student. Studying law also means learning to be a complete human being: thinking, feeling, and acting with balance. Good law is not only just in text but also acceptable to the community's sense of justice. This is where law must align with culture.

A cultured nation is a nation that knows itself. And it's impossible for someone to become a wise legal expert if they don't recognize their own social and cultural roots. Therefore, the ideal process of learning law should not only take place in the classroom, but also within society—hearing voices often silenced, witnessing events undocumented, and exploring values passed down through word of mouth, symbols, and tradition.

Just as the macapat song embodies the philosophy of life from birth to death, legal knowledge should not only address the questions of today, but also serve as a bridge between generations: past, present, and future. If we want to create a legal system that favors humanity, then humanity itself—with all its cultural complexity—must be re-positioned as the center of the legal learning process.

Local wisdom is inseparable from our legal identity as a nation. Javanese culture, for example, teaches important concepts such as rukun (harmony), tepa slira (compassion), and samadya (compassion)—values that can serve as fundamental principles for resolving conflicts without violence and through a family-like approach. In Javanese society, dispute resolution does not always have to end up in court. Many conflicts are resolved through village-level deliberation, family discussions, or the intervention of community leaders. Here, the law is not merely a text, but lives as a social process that maintains harmony.

Unfortunately, the current legal education system often places culture as merely an accessory, not a foundation. Yet, to become a sensitive lawyer, not only adept at speaking in court but also able to read the silent language of the people, it is crucial for us to see law as the product of cultural, historical, and social structural relationships. This is why studying law must be more than just reading a book—it must be an exercise in understanding people, society, and meaning.

As a formerly colonized nation, historical experiences and collective trauma must also be part of how we view the law. Javanese culture, often perceived as passive, actually harbors tensions, coping strategies, and even resistance hidden in symbols and traditions. When we understand this, we will see that defending justice is not only about fighting for what is right in formal law, but also about giving voice to those long silenced by a system that has never been fully just.

So, in studying law, let's acknowledge that not everything can be explained by black-and-white norms. Behind a legal conflict may be hidden traces of colonialism, cultural wounds, or unresolved value struggles. And a lawyer's job is not merely to read the law, but also to translate social reality into a legal framework that favors substantive justice.

A prospective lawyer rooted in the nation's soul cannot rely solely on dry, technocratic Western formal legal values. He or she needs to practice listening to the pulse of his or her community—especially those who are least given a voice. In Javanese culture, we learn to grasp the meaning of the unspoken, to understand the implicit meaning more deeply than the explicit. This is not merely politeness, but part of a rich value system that can inform our methodology for resolving legal issues fairly and humanely.

For example, in resolving land disputes, we cannot simply rely on article-by-article logic if we don't understand the meaning of land for indigenous communities as an ancestral heritage, not simply an asset. Or in cases of domestic violence, an overly formal legal approach can fail to capture the complexities of a culture of silence and the sense of "shyness" that discourages victims from speaking out. Here, a culture-based approach is crucial: we must build empathy, not just argument.

Furthermore, a culture-based legal approach should not be dismissed as outdated or unscientific. It is precisely from there that we can build a contextual legal system—one that addresses the real needs of society. We need more lawyers, judges, prosecutors, and legal academics who understand that justice is not simply a black-and-white decision in a courtroom, but rather a long-term process that must be rooted in the nation's soul.

Studying law rooted in the spirit of the Javanese nation and culture means embracing local wisdom as an instrument of justice, not merely an academic tool. This is where "rasa"—a Javanese concept that teaches intuition, inner awareness, and ethical precision in interpreting situations—is crucial. A legal expert who is able to feel, not just calculate and interpret articles, will be more sensitive to unheard suffering and unspoken wounds.

The value of "tep selira", or tolerance, for example, is not only a social principle, but also a method for navigating legal conflicts. In many disputes, wise resolution does not come from who is most correct according to positive law, but rather who is best able to understand and restore fractured social relations. That's where Javanese culture gives us direction: justice is not just about winners and losers, but about restoration and balance.

Unfortunately, this approach is often considered too lenient in modern legal systems that prioritize procedural efficiency. However, if we open a dialogue between cultural values and legal logic, a more humanistic approach to law will emerge—one that balances logic and feeling, certainty and wisdom. This doesn't mean rejecting progress, but rather rooting it more deeply so that we are not uprooted from the very soil of justice itself.

In Javanese society, the law isn't always spoken, but it is felt. It manifests itself in behavior, actions, and speech. Javanese people don't always say "this is wrong," but can point out irregularities through silence, a look, or a detached attitude. This is where it's crucial to understand that learning about law isn't solely from books, articles, or jurisprudence, but also from the social order that has been managing conflict for hundreds of years through symbolic and meaningful means.

When someone is humiliated not through insults, but through symbols—such as being uninvited to a feast or being unwelcome at a village market—then an informal legal process is actually taking place. Social sanctions shape behavior, even more effective than mere fines or punishments. These sanctions are unwritten, but obeyed out of shame and respect—two qualities often absent from modern courtrooms.

Conversely, when state law exists only as rules without understanding the structure of societal sentiment, it can feel alien, rigid, and even colonial. This is where law, divorced from culture, fails to fully understand human needs. Therefore, learning law from the spirit of one's own nation—in this case, Javanese culture—is an effort to restore the spirit of justice to its origins: not on paper, but in the hearts and lives of the people.

Learning from Javanese culture also means accepting that not everything can be resolved through force or punishment. There are times when mediation is wiser than the courts, there are times when silence is nobler than debate, and there are times when justice is achieved not by someone winning, but by all parties recovering. This kind of law is not only just, but also wise.

And perhaps that's what's forgotten today: that studying law isn't just about winning in court, but also about being a just, wise, and grounded human being. Javanese culture teaches that true justice isn't just about upholding the law, but about respecting people—with feeling, with courtesy, with a balance of certainty and wisdom.

# Closing

## Sowing Law from Cultural Roots

Law isn't something that falls from the sky. It grows, spreads, and shapes itself from the way people live and interact in society. In the Indonesian context, particularly in Java, law grows from rice paddies, from hermitages, from songs, from parental advice, from the silent cries of a mother, and from the silent actions of a father who chooses to give in for the sake of harmony.

When we study laws rooted in our own culture, we not only gain knowledge but also rediscover who we are. Justice is not merely the result of a trial, but a feeling cultivated in everyday life. Laws that fail to understand culture will be fragile; they are like tall trees with shallow roots, easily toppled by the winds of time.

In today's fast-paced and viral world, we need to return to our roots. This isn't to reject progress, but to ensure our steps remain firm and grounded. Javanese culture, with all its wisdom, teaches us an important lesson: that being right isn't enough; we must also be wise. That winning doesn't always mean fairness. That silence is sometimes more powerful than shouting.

As lawyers, as citizens, and as human beings, let us learn law not only from the statute books, but also from the soul of the nation. From the common people who daily create order through politeness, from puppeteers who convey criticism through plays, and from villages that preserve values when the city begins to forget them.

This book is an invitation. Not to romanticize the past, but to courageously present a future of law with a soul that is not uprooted from the soil in which it was born. For true law is not merely that which can conquer, but that which can heal.

**In conclusion, true justice is not just about what is written in the articles, but about how we humanize humans.**

Thank you for reading. May this book be a small part of our long journey to uphold just, humane, and cultured laws.

# Thank-you note

**Thank God**Praise be to Allah SWT, who has given me the strength, health, and time to write and complete this book with full sincerity. Without His permission, all my efforts would be meaningless.

I express my deepest gratitude to my beloved family, who have been a source of encouragement and peace of mind throughout the process of writing this book. I extend my deepest appreciation to the teachers, lecturers, and elders whose knowledge I have absorbed, both in silence and through discussions.

I would also like to express my thanks to my colleagues, initial readers, editors, and all parties who have provided input, criticism, and encouragement in improving this manuscript.

Especially for the Javanese and Indonesian people whose stories have inspired many, and all the justice seekers who have silently taught the meaning of struggle — I dedicate this book.

Hopefully this work will be of ongoing benefit, bringing light to understanding for those who read it, and becoming a continuous charity for the author.

Biodata

# About the Author

**Muhammad Ari Pratomo**, which is widely known by the name**Muhammad Ari Law**, born on**June 21, 1982**. a**Indonesian Lawyer**,**legal aid activist**, and a public figure who has consistently defended the interests of the common people since the year**2009**. he expanded his service through political channels because of his close involvement with the needs of the community at the grassroots.

# Organizational Achievements and Activities

- Coordinator of Cooperation of DPC PERADI Bekasi (2015–2019)
- Coordinator of the Commercial Sector of the PERADI Bekasi Legal Aid Center (2015–2019)
- Founder & Supervisor of the Tafsir Qolbu Al-Karomah Martial Arts School
- Founder of the Center for Communication, Information and Legal Services
- Supervisor of the Karomallah Banten – Lampung School
- Founder & Initiator of the Indonesian Social Media & Live Streaming Control Institute
- Founder & Initiator of the Indonesian Positive Live Community

## Professional Experience

- **Founder of Law Office ARI PRATOMO & ASSOCIATES** www.aripratomo.com[1]
- **Founder of Media General Infokom**
- **Posbakum Lawyer at Bekasi District Court**
- **Posbakum Lawyer at the East Jakarta District Court**
- **Posbakum Lawyer at the Indonesian Advocates Association, DPC Bandar Lampung**
- Currently active as**Advocates in various fields of law**, both litigation and non-litigation, through its own law firm.

1. http://www.aripratomo.com

# Official Social Media

- **Instagram:** @muhammadarilaw[1]
- **YouTube:** MuhammadAriLaw Channel[2]
- **TikTok:** @muhammadarilaw[3]
- **Twitter (X):** @MuhammadAriLaw[4]
- **LinkedIn:** linkedin.com/in/muhammadarilaw[5]
- **Facebook:**@MuhammadAriLaw

1. https://www.instagram.com/muhammadarilaw
2. https://www.youtube.com/channel/UCSDXD741N2uND_c3TPBVYyg
3. https://www.tiktok.com/@muhammadarilaw?lang=in
4. https://twitter.com/MuhammadAriLaw
5. https://www.linkedin.com/in/muhammadarilaw

# Blurp

# JAVA, JUSTICE, AND THE SOUL OF INDONESIA

*A Lawyer's Guide to Culture, Law, and the Hopes of His Nation*

**"When the law doesn't speak enough, culture will answer."**

In an increasingly cold and formal legal world, Muhammad Ari Pratomo, a lawyer and author, presents a moving book—not just to be understood, but to be felt. He speaks not merely of articles and procedures, but of cultural roots, the conscience of justice, and the soul of a nation wounded but unyielding.

Through a narrative rich in Javanese philosophy, true stories of the community, and poignant reflections on customary law and the courts today, this book is a contemplative guide—for legal thinkers, culture lovers, and anyone who believes that justice should not be separated from humanity.

**JAVA, JUSTICE, AND THE SOUL OF INDONESIA**is a lawyer's conscience for his people. A call to return to the roots, so that the law can grow—not only strong, but also wise.

"This book is more than just a work. It is the soul of Indonesia in terms of noble cultural values, from a child of the nation for his homeland."

**Synopsis**

What would happen if a lawyer didn't just talk about articles and cases, but also explored the philosophy of wayang, Javanese songs, and forgotten village wisdom?

In this book, author Muhammad Ari Pratomo invites us to explore the face of Indonesian law from a rarely explored perspective, encompassing culture, tradition, and the nation's spirit. With a warm and reflective narrative style, he discusses how Javanese values—such as etiquette, the culture of silence, and the spirit of mutual cooperation—meet the rigid and procedural modern legal system.

This book opens the eyes to the fact that justice in Indonesia cannot be measured solely through the courtroom, but also through feelings, history, local wisdom, and culture. Through true stories, the author's experiences as an advocate, and cultural reflections, the author crafts a moral and spiritual guide for anyone seeking to understand Indonesian law from within.

**Suitable for general readers, law students, cultural observers, and anyone who longs for a law that is more humane, down-to-earth, and rooted.**

# Don't miss out!

Visit the website below and you can sign up to receive emails whenever Muhammad Ari Pratomo publishes a new book. There's no charge and no obligation.

https://books2read.com/r/B-A-YQCSD-AOZSG

BOOKS 2 READ

Connecting independent readers to independent writers.

Did you love *JAVANESE JUSTICE AND THE SOUL OF INDONESIA A Lawyer's Guide to Culture, Law, and the Hopes of His Nation*? Then you should read *How to Respect Bali in Its Entirety Binding Legal, Customary, and Mystical Rules Island of the Gods*[1] by Muhammad Ari Pratomo!

[2]

**How to Respect Bali in Its Entirety** *The Legal, Customary, and Mystical Rules that Bind the Island of the Gods* **Works by Muhammad Ari Pratomo**

**Bali is not just a destination—it is a living entity guarded by law, custom, and spiritual forces.** This book is not just reading, but a bridge to understanding the true soul of the Island of the Gods.

1. https://books2read.com/u/mYMkDW
2. https://books2read.com/u/mYMkDW

Whether you are a tourist, expat, investor, or Indonesian citizen looking to live, work, or simply visit Bali—this book will be your ethical and practical compass.

Compiled by Muhammad Ari Pratomo, a lawyer, writer, and cultural observer, this book reveals invisible yet very real boundaries: from legal entanglements to customary curses, from spiritual prohibitions to state laws, from banjar to the invisible energy banar.

**One thing is for sure: Bali will welcome you warmly—if you come with knowledge, humility, and respect.**

**Read this before you venture further into Bali. Because here, every step can mean law, custom, or destiny.**

Read more at https://muhammadarilaw.com.

# Also by Muhammad Ari Pratomo

LEGAL MECHANISMS OF FOREIGN INVESTMENT iN NDONESIA
The Daily Pen of a Lawyer
Foreign Lawyers in Indonesia: Between Global Collaboration and Legal Sovereignty
The Final Judgement
Youth at the End of Time – A Guide to a Broken World
Back to Father's Embrace
How to Respect Bali in Its Entirety Binding Legal, Customary, and Mystical Rules Island of the Gods
JAVANESE JUSTICE AND THE SOUL OF INDONESIA A Lawyer's Guide to Culture, Law, and the Hopes of His Nation

Watch for more at https://muhammadarilaw.com.

# About the Author

**Author ProfileName: Muhammad Ari PratomoOccupation: Lawyer, Writer, SongwriterBorn: Indonesia, June 21, 1982Instagram: @MuhammadAriLawTikTok: @MuhammadAriLawYouTube: @MuhammadAriLawLinkedIn: Muhammad Ari PratomoX (Twitter): @MuhammadAriLaw**

Read more at https://muhammadarilaw.com.

## About the Publisher

**PT MuhammadAriLaw Pustaka Nada**

is a book publisher based in Indonesia, founded by Muhammad Ari Pratomo—a lawyer, writer, and songwriter. The publisher is dedicated to works that voice justice, awaken empathy, and weave the power of law, literature, and conscience into a global literary movement.

Read more at https://mpnpublishing.com.

www.ingramcontent.com/pod-product-compliance
Lightning Source LLC
LaVergne TN
LVHW090422210926
848480LV00002B/658